MERE MORTALS

MORTALS

Six One-Act Comedies

by DAVID IVES

★

DRAMATISTS
PLAY SERVICE
INC.

TABLE OF CONTENTS

MERE MORTALS

ACT ONE

ACT TWO

MERE MORTALS received its premiere at Primary Stages Company (Casey Childs, Artistic Director) in New York City, in May, 1997. The evening was directed by John Rando; the set design was by Russell Metheny; the costume design was by Anita Yavich; the lighting design was by Phil Monat; the sound design was by Aural Fixation; and the stage manager was Christine Catti. The cast was as follows:

ACTOR ONE...Willis Sparks
ACTOR TWO ....Arnie Burton
ACTOR THREE ....Danton Stone
ACTRESS ONE ....Jessalyn Gilsig
ACTRESS TWO... Nancy Opel
ACTRESS THREE .... Anne O'Sullivan

MERE MORTALS can be performed with six actors (3 men, 3 women) taking the following parts:

ACTOR ONE: FOREPLAY, Chuck I; MERE MORTALS, Joe; TIME FLIES, David Attenborough; SPEED-THE-PLAY, Teach, Fox, Danny; DEGAS, C'EST MOI, Driver, Key Food Worker, OTB Worker, Museum Guard

ACTOR TWO: FOREPLAY, Chuck II; MERE MORTALS, Frank; TIME FLIES, Horace; SPEED-THE-PLAY, Bobby, John; DR. FRITZ, Tom; DEGAS, C'EST MOI, Newsguy, Renoir

ACTOR THREE: FOREPLAY, Chuck III; MERE MORTALS, Charlie; SPEED-THE-PLAY, Don, Gould, Bernie; DEGAS, C'EST MOI, Ed

ACTRESS ONE: FOREPLAY, Amy; SPEED-THE-PLAY, Carol, Karen, Deborah; DEGAS, C'EST MOI, Young Woman

ACTRESS TWO: FOREPLAY, Annie; SPEED-THE-PLAY, M.C.; DR. FRITZ, Maria/Dr. Fritz; DEGAS, C'EST MOI, Doris, Homeless Person, Twin Donut Worker

ACTRESS THREE: FOREPLAY, Alma; TIME FLIES, May; SPEED-THE-PLAY, Joan; DEGAS, C'EST MOI, Dry Cleaning Woman, Unemployment Worker; Librarian; Museumgoer

MERE MORTALS

ACT ONE

FOREPLAY
Or: The Art of the Fugue

Revised Edition

this play is for Bennett Cohen

FOREPLAY: OR THE ART OF THE FUGUE was originally presented in somewhat different form at the Manhattan Punch
Line Theatre (Steve Kaplan, Artistic Director) in New York City,
in February, 1991. It was directed by Jason McConnell Buzas;
the set design was by Vaughn Patterson; the costume design
was by Kitty Leech; the lighting design was by Pat Dignan. The
cast was as follows:

AMY .... Laura Dean
CHUCK .... Robert Stanton
ANNIE .... Alison Martin
CHUCK II .... Tony Carlin
ALMA .... Anne O'Sullivan
CHUCK III .... Brian Howe

CHARACTERS

AMY — early 20s, very sweet
CHUCK I — early 20s, very charming
ANNIE — mid-20s, very wry
CHUCK II — mid-20s, very smooth
ALMA — any age from early 20s to 30s; very sexy
CHUCK III — late 20s (or more), pretty tired

All three Chuck's are dressed exactly the same.

SETTING

A bare stage representing a miniature-golf course. Upstage, a miniature castle/windmill. Hanging over the action: a sign that says "LILLI-PUTT LANE."

NOTE: Actual golf balls are not used, but mimed.

FOREPLAY
Or: The Art of the Fugue

At lights up: Chuck I and Amy, with golf clubs.

CHUCK I. *FORE!*

AMY. I can't believe I'm out here.

CHUCK I. Amy, you are going to fall in love tonight.

AMY. I am?

CHUCK I. With miniature golf.

AMY. Chuck ...

CHUCK I. I swear. This night will turn you into a minia-ture-golf-o-*maniac.* You're going to like this game so much, you'll wake up shorter tomorrow.

AMY. Very cute.

CHUCK I. It's an elevating experience.

AMY. Very funny.

CHUCK I. Just remember one thing: miniature golf is big-ger than you or me.

AMY. You must be some kind of a charmer, to talk me into this.

CHUCK I. Now why don't you take your best shot and just try to resist. Go on.

AMY. Okay ...

CHUCK I. *(As she hits the "ball.")* Puck! *(As it travels.)* Aaaaaaaaaaaaaaaand — *(It misses.)* Ouch.

AMY. Ohhhhhhhhhhhh ... *(This disappointed, fading moan is the sound that Amy will typically make when she misses a shot.)*

CHUCK I. Too bad. Did you know, by the way, that a race of dwarves once covered the earth? This — *(The miniature wind-mill.)* — is what they left behind.

AMY. Ha, ha.

CHUCK I. This was their Stonehenge.

AMY.   Did you just think of this?

CHUCK I.   You didn't know that but it's true.

AMY.   Did you just make that up?

CHUCK I.   But please. Take another shot.

AMY.   I don't know how I got into this.

CHUCK I.   *(As she putts again.)* Puck! Aaaaaaaaaaaand — *Ouch.*

AMY.   *(Missing.)* Ohhhhhhhhhh ...

CHUCK I.   Nice bounce. But no cigar.

AMY.   It wasn't a *bad* shot.

CHUCK I.   Anyway, that's why I come out here to Lilli-Putt Lane. To sense a cosmic bond with the ancient practitioners of the game.

AMY.   Uh-huh. And to seduce girls.

CHUCK I.   *What?!*

AMY.   Oh come on, Chuck.

CHUCK I.   What guy in his right mind would take a girl miniature-golfing to seduce her?

AMY.   You would. You've got quite a reputation, you know.

CHUCK I.   What, "reputation"?

AMY.   *Don Juan.*

CHUCK I.   Amy, I swear. I've never taken a girl miniature-golfing in my life. Or anybody *else's* life!

AMY.   Uh-huh.

CHUCK I.   But do you want to take your next shot? Or do you want to resign right now?

AMY.   If this is about getting into bed with me ...

CHUCK I.   Never in a million years.

AMY.   You can think again.

CHUCK I.   *(As she putts.)* Puck! Aaaaaaaaaaaaaaaaaand —

AMY.   *(As it goes in.) Yes!*

CHUCK I.   Hey! That was good, Amy!

AMY.   That was good, wasn't it?

CHUCK I.   That was *very* good.

AMY.   Wow! That felt great!

CHUCK I.   It's almost an erotic thrill, isn't it? *(Off her look.)* I take it back. It's not an erotic thrill. It's a mild celibate *frisson.*

AMY.   You are shameless.

CHUCK I. *(Getting ready to putt.)* Quiet, please. I'm concentrating here. *(He tees off.) Puck!*

AMY *(As the ball travels.)* Mmmmmmmmmmmmmmmmmmmmmmmmmm — !

CHUCK I. *(Overlapping that.)* Aaaaaaaaaaaaaaaaaaaaaaand ... *(The ball goes in.)* BINGO!

AMY. Wow!

CHUCK I. Am I good?

AMY. That was nice!

CHUCK I. Am I good?

AMY. You're really good.

CHUCK I. Okay. Let's put this down for infinity. *(Marks a scorecard.)* Three for Amy. And a hole in one ... for Chuck.

AMY. God. It takes so little, doesn't it.

CHUCK I. So little?

AMY. To make people happy. It takes so little for happiness.

CHUCK I. And what is littler than miniature golf? So are you getting interested? Shall we play on?

AMY. Yeah. Let's play on.

CHUCK I. *FORE!*

CHUCK II. *(Offstage.) FORE! (Chuck II enters with Annie at the first hole as Chuck I and Amy move on to the second hole.)*

ANNIE. Chuck, they ought to lock you up.

CHUCK II. What...?

ANNIE. You are *shameless,* Chuck.

CHUCK II. Annie, what are you talking about?

CHUCK I. You know, I once played miniature golf with Dustin Hoffman?

AMY. With Dustin Hoffman?

ANNIE. I'm supposed to believe you?

CHUCK I. He's so short it was pretty miniature already.

AMY. Ha, ha.

ANNIE. Ha, ha.

CHUCK II. Annie, I've never taken a girl miniature golfing in my life!

ANNIE. I'll bet.

CHUCK II. I swear!

CHUCK I. I swear!

CHUCK II.   Or anybody *else's* life!

AMY.   Uh-huh.

ANNIE.   With your reputation?

CHUCK II.   What reputation?

ANNIE.   *Don Juan.*

CHUCK II.   Oh Amy, Amy. You have to learn to trust people.

CHUCK I.   *(As Amy gets ready to tee off again.)* Trust yourself, now.

ANNIE.   Annie.

CHUCK II.   Excuse me?

ANNIE.   My name is Annie. You called me Amy.

CHUCK II.   I'm sorry. *Annie.*

ANNIE.   I'm going to keep my eye on you.

CHUCK I.   *(To Amy.)* Just keep your eye on the ball.

CHUCK II.   Annie-way — prepare to fall in love tonight. With miniature golf.

ANNIE.   Oh yes?

CHUCK II.   It's an elevating experience. And bigger than you or me.

ANNIE.   Very clever. I just hope nobody sees me out here.

CHUCK I and CHUCK II.   *(As Amy and Annie tee off.) Puck!*

CHUCK II.   Aaaaaaaaand ...

CHUCK I.   Aaaaaaaaaaaaand ...

AMY.   Mmmmmmmmmmmmmmmmmm ...

ANNIE.   *(Her typical sound, at missing a shot.) Nyugh!*

AMY.   Ohhhhhhhhhh ...

CHUCK I.   Too bad.

CHUCK II.   Nice lay, though.

CHUCK I.   Very nice lay.

CHUCK II.   *(Off Annie's look.)* It's just a *golfing* term.

CHUCK I.   It's perfectly innocent.

AMY and ANNIE.   I'm sure. *(The women get ready to putt again.)*

CHUCK II.   Did you know, by the way, that a race of dwarves once covered the earth? This is what they left behind.

ANNIE.   Ha, ha.

CHUCK II.   This was their Stonehenge.

ANNIE.   Very cute.

CHUCK II.   You didn't know that but it's true.

AMY.   I know you're only trying to distract me.

ANNIE.   You're not going to distract me.

CHUCK II.   Puck!

CHUCK I.   Puck!

CHUCK I and CHUCK II.   Aaaaaaaaaaaaand —

CHUCK II.   *(As Annie misses.)* BONG.

ANNIE.   *Nyugh!*

CHUCK I.   BONG.

AMY.   Ohhhhhhhhhhhh ...

CHUCK II.   Anyway, that's why I come out here. To sense a connection with my shorter predecessors.

AMY.   Did you just make all that up?

ANNIE.   Does somebody write all this for you?

CHUCK I and CHUCK II.   What?

AMY.   Golfing with Dustin Hoffman.

ANNIE.   A midget Stonehenge.

CHUCK II.   I don't make anything up.

CHUCK I.   This is truth!

ANNIE.   You do have ...

AMY.   There is something about you ...

ANNIE.   ... charm. I guess.

AMY.   But you sure have a way of making everything mean something else.

CHUCK I.   And that's what's great about miniature golf.

CHUCK II.   You know what I like about this game?

CHUCK I.   It means something else.

CHUCK II.   It's a metaphor.

CHUCK I.   It's a great metaphor.

ANNIE.   Okay. A metaphor.

AMY and ANNIE.   What for?

AMY.   *I* know.

ANNIE.   For sex.

AMY.   For seduction.

CHUCK I.   No —

CHUCK II.   No —

ANNIE.   Sure! "Keeping *score*."

AMY.   "Getting it in the *hole*."

CHUCK I.   No —

CHUCK II.   No —

CHUCK I.   No! It's a metaphor for life!

CHUCK II.   For death.

ANNIE.   Did you say "for *death?*"

CHUCK II.   Those aren't just holes out there.

CHUCK I.   Those are stages on the journey of life.

CHUCK II.   The course always leads to the same final place.

CHUCK I.   And the way is different for everybody.

CHUCK II.   Sandtraps.

CHUCK I.   Waterholes.

CHUCK II.   The sands of time.

CHUCK I.   The oases of purification.

CHUCK II.   The final hole.

CHUCK I.   The verdant fairways ...

AMY.   What a beautiful idea!

ANNIE.   What a crock of manure!

CHUCK I.   And I believe it.

ANNIE.   Right. The five stages of miniature golf: anger, de-
nial, grief, blame — and a windmill.

CHUCK II.   That's good, Amy.

CHUCK I.   You're a good person.

ANNIE.   Annie.

CHUCK II.   Annie.

CHUCK I.   Amy.

CHUCK II.   Maybe you fear the challenge of miniature golf.

ANNIE.   I fear the challenge of miniature *men.*

CHUCK I.   So do you want to play on, or...?

CHUCK II.   Do you want to resign?

ANNIE.   No.

AMY.   Yeah.

AMY and ANNIE.   Let's play on.

CHUCK II.   Good.

CHUCK I and CHUCK II.   *(As the women putt.)* Puck!

CHUCK I.   Aaaaaaaaand ...

CHUCK II.   Aaaaaaaaaaaand ...

AMY.   *(Joining in, overlapping.)* Mmmmmmmmmmmmmmmmmmmm ...

ANNIE.   *(Joining in, overlapping.)* Uhhhhhhhhhhhhhhhhhhhhh-

18

hhhhhh ...

AMY and ANNIE. *YES!*

CHUCK II. Nice shot.

CHUCK I. Nice shot.

AMY. Boy, that felt good!

ANNIE. Whoo!

AMY. Well!

ANNIE. Wow. Thought I wasn't up to it, huh.

AMY. It really *is* an erotic thrill, isn't it?

CHUCK II. Okay.

CHUCK I. You want to see an erotic thrill?

CHUCK II. Watch this.

CHUCK I. Watch this.

CHUCK I and CHUCK II. *(As they tee off, a soft sexual moan.)*
Puck. (As the ball travels, the orgasm grows.)

CHUCK I. Oh, yes ...

CHUCK II. Yes ...

AMY. Mmmmmmmmmmmmmmmm ...

CHUCK I. *Yes...!*

ANNIE. Ohhhhhhhhhh ...

CHUCK II. Yes!

CHUCK I. YES!

AMY and ANNIE. OHHHHHHHHHHHH!

CHUCK II. *YES!*

CHUCK I. *YES!*

CHUCK I and CHUCK II. *BINGO! (All four: collective fading
post-orgasmic moan.)*

AMY. Boy! Nice shot!

CHUCK I. Am I good?

CHUCK II. Am I good?

ANNIE. You're good, all right.

AMY. You're very good.

CHUCK II. Okay.

CHUCK I. Okay.

CHUCK II. Let's put this down for infinity. *(The two Chucks
mark their scorecards.)* A hole in one ...

CHUCK I. Another hole in one ...

CHUCK I and CHUCK II. For Chuck.

CHUCK II. So are you enjoying yourself?

AMY. I'm having a very good time.

ANNIE. I am enjoying myself, in spite of myself.

CHUCK II. You know it takes so little, to make people happy. Amy —

ANNIE. Annie.

CHUCK II. Annie ...

CHUCK I. Amy, have you ever thought there's a design in our lives?

CHUCK II. Maybe there's something bigger than all this.

ANNIE. Polo?

AMY. *I* think so.

CHUCK II. And you could be a part of it.

CHUCK I. You could be a part of some greater design in my life.

CHUCK II. You're so ...

CHUCK I. You're so ...

CHUCK II. ... different.

CHUCK I. ... different, somehow.

CHUCK II. You're not just ... Annie-body.

ANNIE. Ha, ha.

CHUCK II. You know the night is young ...

CHUCK I. The stars are out.

CHUCK II. We could forget golf.

CHUCK I. We could go over to my place.

ANNIE. And chuck the game?

AMY. Why don't we see who wins first.

ANNIE. Let's play on a little.

CHUCK I. Okay.

CHUCK I and II. *FORE!*

CHUCK III. *(Offstage.) FORE! (Chuck III enters with Alma.)* Do you know I've never taken a girl miniature golfing before?

ALMA. Oh yeah, how come? I been on lots of miniature golf dates. *(That stops Chuck III, a little.)*

CHUCK III. Oh, really...?

ALMA. Sure, I love miniature golf. I play it all the time.

CHUCK III. *(Not too heartily.)* Well great. That's terrific.

ALMA.   It's kind of an elevating experience. You want to go first?

CHUCK III.   Uh — no. Be my guest.

CHUCK II.   Did I tell you that I once played miniature golf with Dustin Hoffman?

ANNIE.   Dustin Hoffman.

CHUCK II.   Yeah. It's pretty miniature with Dusty.

ANNIE.   Ha, ha.

CHUCK I.   *(Clearing his throat.)* Hem, hem.

AMY.   I know you're only trying to distract me.

CHUCK II.   *Hem, hem.*

ANNIE.   Very cute. May I play on?

CHUCK II.   Please.

CHUCK III.   Did you know, by the way, that a race of dwarves once covered the earth?

ALMA.   They *DID?*

CHUCK III.   Well ...

ALMA.   *Dwarfs?*

CHUCK III.   Not really.

ALMA.   You mean midgets were like all over the world?

CHUCK III.   I was only kidding, actually.

ALMA.   Oh boy, you had me scared! But I bet if that was really true, they probably would've left something like this behind, huh? Like *Stonehenge* or something.

CHUCK III.   Yeah.

ALMA.   Wouldn't that be funny?

CHUCK III.   Mm. Hysterical.

ANNIE.   Why don't *you* go first.

AMY.   *You* go first this time.

CHUCK I.   All right.

CHUCK II.   Gladly.

CHUCK III.   Just remember: this game is bigger than you or me.

ALMA.   Huh?

CHUCK III.   It's *bigger* than us. You know — *bigger...?*

ALMA.   Oh. It's "bigger" than us.

CHUCK III.   Yeah. "Bigger." Just a little joke. *(Chuck I, Chuck II and Alma line up to tee off.)*

21

AMY.   *(Clearing her throat.)* Hem.

ANNIE.   *(Clearing her throat.)* Hem.

CHUCK II.   That's not going to work, you know.

AMY.   *(As Chuck I putts.)* Puck!

ANNIE.   *(As Chuck II putts.)* Puck!

CHUCK III.   *(As Alma putts.)* Puck!

CHUCKS I, II, and III.   Aaaaaaaaaaaaaaand …

CHUCK I.   *(Misses.)* Oof.

CHUCK II.   *(Misses.)* Ouch.

AMY and ANNIE.   BONG.

ALMA.   *YES!* A HOLE IN *ONE! WHOOOOO!*

ANNIE.   Too bad.

AMY.   Nice try, though.

ALMA.   Was that good?

CHUCK III.   That was good, Amy.

ALMA.   Alma.

CHUCK III.   Huh?

ALMA.   My name is Alma, you called me Amy.

CHUCK III.   Oh. Sorry.

ALMA.   No problem. Wanna shoot?

AMY and ANNIE.   *(As Chuck I and II putt again.)* Puck!

CHUCK I and II.   Aaaaaaaaaaaaaaand … .

CHUCK III.   You know what I like about miniature golf?

ALMA.   The metaphor?

AMY and ANNIE.   BONG.

ANNIE.   Too bad.

ALMA.   Do you like the life metaphor or the death metaphor?

CHUCK III.   Uh — well. Never mind.

AMY.   Nice try.

ALMA.   I just like this 'cause it's fun. Like sex or something. You wanna … shoot?

CHUCK III.   Sure.

ANNIE.   *(As Chuck II putts.)* Puck!

AMY.   *(As Chuck I putts.)* Puck!

CHUCK III.   *(Putting.)* Puck!

CHUCK I.   *(Dully.)* And —

CHUCK II.   *(Not much verve.)* Bingo. *(Alma: raspberry.)*

AMY.   I wouldn't worry about it.

ANNIE. You're right on par for the hole. *(Amy, Annie and Chuck III get ready to putt.)*

ALMA. You've got quite a reputation, you know.

CHUCK III. What reputation ...

ALMA. As a Donald Juan.

CHUCK III. Oh. A *Donald* Juan.

CHUCK I. *(As Amy putts.)* Puck.

AMY. *Yes!*

CHUCK II. *(As Annie putts.)* Puck.

ANNIE. Excellent!

CHUCK III. *(As he putts.)* Puck.

ALMA. *(Raspberry.)* And what a lousy lay. That's a golfing term.

ANNIE and AMY. Scorecard, please. *(Chucks I and II hand over their scorecards.)*

CHUCK III. You know I once played miniature golf with Dustin Hoffman?

ALMA. Musta been pretty miniature, he's so short.

CHUCK III. Look, we haven't gone out *before,* have we?

ALMA. No.

CHUCK III. I mean, we haven't played this course before, have we?

ALMA. I don't think so.

AMY and ANNIE. FORE!

CHUCK I. So anyway.

CHUCK II. What's your story, Annie?

CHUCK I. What's your background?

CHUCK III. Got any family?

AMY. I have two brothers.

ANNIE. Three sisters.

ALMA. Two brothers, a sister, a step-sister, a half-brother, and my dog Barky.

CHUCKS I, II and III. Uh-huh.

CHUCK I. *(As he putts.)* Puck.

CHUCK II. *(As he putts.)* Puck.

CHUCK III. *(As he putts.)* Puck.

ALMA. Do you have to make those noises?

CHUCK I. Ouch.

CHUCK II. Oof.

AMY and ANNIE. *BONG.*

CHUCK III. What noises?

ALMA. You make noises while you golf.

CHUCK III. Oh. Sorry.

ALMA. Your shot again, Dick.

CHUCK III. It's *Chuck,* actually.

ALMA. Oh. Sorry. *(Chucks I, II and III prepare to putt again.)*

AMY. Anyway ...

ANNIE. My mother's dead.

AMY. My father lives in Arkansas.

ALMA. My brother is an undertaker.

CHUCK I and CHUCK II. Puck!

AMY and ANNIE. Aaaaaaaaaaaaaand —

ALMA. My sister is a dike.

AMY and ANNIE. *BONG! (As Chuck III misses, Alma: raspberry.)*

CHUCK III. You know, *you* make noises too.

ALMA. I do?

CHUCK III. Oh yeah.

ALMA. Funny. *I* never noticed. *(As Chucks I, II and III putt.)*

AMY and ANNIE. Puck!

CHUCK I and II. Aaaaaaaaaaaaaand — !

AMY, ANNIE, CHUCKS I and II. BINGO! *(Alma: raspberry.)*

CHUCK III. I can't hit the ball if I don't go "puck."

ALMA. "Puck?"

CHUCK III. I have to make a noise.

ALMA. Go ahead. Make all the noise you want.

CHUCK I. *(Referring to Chuck III.)* Looks like we've got a real moron up ahead here.

CHUCK III. *(Feeling Alma watching him.)* You're not going to make me miss my shot.

ALMA. It's two inches away! Just hit it!

CHUCK I and II. *Playing through!*

CHUCK III. Puck.

CHUCK I and II. *Playing through!*

CHUCK III. And bingo.

AMY. Okay, now.

ANNIE. This is war.

CHUCKS I and II, AMY and ANNIE. *(As Amy and Annie putt.)*
Puck!
CHUCK I and II. Aaaaaaaaaaaaand …
AMY and ANNIE. All right!
CHUCKS I and II, AMY and ANNIE. *(As Chuck I, Chuck II, and Alma putt.)* Puck!
AMY and ANNIE. Aaaaaaaaaaaaaaand … .
CHUCK I and II. BINGO!
ALMA. *Yes! ANOTHER HOLE IN ONE! WHOOOO!* Wanna shoot, uh …
CHUCK III. Chuck!
CHUCK I and AMY. Puck!
AMY. Ohhh …
CHUCK II and ANNIE. Puck!
ANNIE. Nyugh!
ALMA. Pork! *(Raspberry.)*
CHUCK III. It's not "pork." It's *"puck."*
ALMA. Oh. Sorry. *(The next six lines very very fast and even.)*
CHUCK I. Puck —
CHUCK II. Puck —
CHUCK I. Puck —
CHUCK II. Puck —
CHUCK I. Puck —
CHUCK II. Puck —
CHUCKS I, II, III, AMY and ANNIE. *(Operatic, Wagnerian.)*
PUCK!
CHUCK I. Ouch.
CHUCK II. Oof.
ANNIE. Nyugh.
AMY. Yes.
CHUCK I and II. Bingo!
ANNIE. Aaaaaaaaaaaand …
AMY. Aaaaaaaaaaaaaand …
CHUCK I. Aaaaaaaaaaaaaaaaand …
CHUCK II. Aaaaaaaaaaaaaaaaaaaaand … *(Alma: Raspberry. The next six lines very very fast and even.)*
CHUCK I. Puck —
CHUCK II. Puck —

CHUCK I. Puck —

CHUCK II. Puck —

CHUCK I. Puck —

CHUCK II. Puck —

CHUCK I and II, AMY and ANNIE. *(Wagnerian.)* PUCK!

CHUCK II. Ouch.

CHUCK I. Oof.

ANNIE. Yes!

AMY. Ohhhhhhh...! *(Crescendo to very loud.)*

CHUCK II. Aaaaaaaand ...

CHUCK I. Aaaaaaaaaaand ...

AMY. Mmmmmmmmmmmmmmmm ...

ANNIE. Mmmmmmmmmmmmmmmmmmm ...

CHUCK I and II. AAAAAAAAAAAAAAAAAAAAAAND —

AMY and ANNIE. MMMMMMMMMMMMMMMMMMMM —

CHUCK III. *(Quietly.)* Bingo.

CHUCK I, II, AMY, ANNIE and ALMA. YES!

AMY. You win. *(Falls into his arms.)*

ANNIE. You lose. *(Shows him the scorecard.)*

ALMA. You wanna fuck?

CHUCK III. Not really.

BLACKOUT

PROPERTY LIST

Golf clubs (CHUCK I, AMY, CHUCK II, ANNIE, CHUCK III,
    ALMA)
Score cards (CHUCK I, CHUCK II, ANNIE)

MERE MORTALS

Revised Edition

this play is in memory
of my father

MERE MORTALS was first presented, in somewhat different form, at Ensemble Studio Theatre (Curt Dempster, Artistic Director) in New York City, in June, 1990. The director was Jason McConnell Buzas; the set design was by Linda Giering Balmuth; the lighting design was by Greg MacPherson; and the costume design was by Leslie McGovern. The cast was as follows:

JOE .... Robert Pastorelli
CHARLIE .... Brian Smiar
FRANK .... Anthony LaPaglia

SETTING

A girder on the 50th floor of a new, unfinished skyscraper. One end of the girder is still unattached and hanging in open space.

CHARACTERS

Charlie, Frank and Joe are construction workers. Joe and Frank are in their thirties. Charlie is in his fifties.

MERE MORTALS

Joe is sitting astride the girder near its attached end. He is unwrapping a sandwich and reading a newspaper with intense absorption.

A bird sails by. Joe doesn't notice. A couple of small clouds sail by. Joe doesn't notice. He looks up, struck by something in the paper.

JOE.   Unbelievable.

CHARLIE.   *(Offstage, singing.)* "I'm the man...!" *(Charlie and Frank enter, carrying lunch pails. Charlie stops, to belt the end of his song.)* "I'm the man! I'm the man I'm the man I'm the man! I'm the man who broke the bank at Monte Carlo!" *(He heads onwards, to the end of the girder.)* Hey, Joe.

JOE.   Hey, Charlie.

FRANK.   Hey, Joe.

JOE.   Hey, Frank. *(Charlie goes out to the very end of the girder and stands looking out. Frank sits midway on the girder and opens his lunch pail.)*

CHARLIE.   You guys think we're gonna make fifty today?

FRANK.   Sure looks like it.

CHARLIE.   Fifty stories down, fifty stories to go.

JOE.   Very momentous.

CHARLIE.   And what a view to have lunch by, huh.

FRANK.   Beautiful.

CHARLIE.   Jersey.

FRANK.   Yeah.

CHARLIE.   My home. *(Humming his song, Charlie sits on the very end of the beam, and opens his lunch pail.)* So. What's the bill of fare today? Frankie, whaddya got?

FRANK.   *(Peering into his sandwich.)* I think it's liverwurst.

CHARLIE.   Joey? Howbout you?

JOE.   *(Reading.)* Pickle and pimento loaf.

FRANK. *(Looking into his sandwich again.)* Wait a minute. This ain't liverwurst. It's tuna. I think … *(Sniffs it.)*

CHARLIE. Well *I* got corned beef and pastrami today.

FRANK. Charlie, is that tuna, or is that liverwurst? *(Realizing.)* Wait, wait, wait. You got corned *beef*?

CHARLIE. And Poupon mustard. The good stuff.

FRANK. On a normal Tuesday? What's the occasion?

CHARLIE. Who says there's an occasion?

FRANK. You hear that, Joe? Charlie's got corned beef and pastrami.

CHARLIE. With Poupon mustard.

FRANK. With Poupon mustard.

JOE. I'm ecstatic. *(A little cloud passes by in the distance.)*

CHARLIE. Oh man, will you look at those poor souls down there, gotta eat their lunch at sea level. *(Sings.)* "I'm the man! I'm the man who broke the bank at Monte Carlo!"

FRANK. So what's the news today, Joe? Some kinda international developments? What's the news from the Ukraine?

JOE. The news today is that a woman in Astoria Queens lived with a guy for *sixteen years,* didn't know the man had five other wives.

FRANK. You hear this, Charlie?

CHARLIE. Many impossible things are actually possible in this world.

FRANK. A guy with six wives — you still call that bigamy?

JOE. No, you call that geometry.

FRANK. That's funny. Well gimme the TV page, will you? Let's see what's on the tube. *(Frank takes TV pages.)*

CHARLIE. Hey, hey, hey. Don't let me hear nothin' about TV. We got bowling tonight.

FRANK. I just want to see what I'm missing.

CHARLIE. And who's in for tonight?

FRANK. I'm in.

CHARLIE. Joe, are you in for tonight?

JOE. I can't this week, Charlie. I got some things I gotta do at home.

CHARLIE. What, you gotta put out some doilies in your wife's powder room or something?

JOE. I got some things I gotta do at home.

CHARLIE. So do 'em tomorrow.

JOE. I can't do 'em tomorrow. Bridget wants me to do 'em tonight.

CHARLIE. Hey, who's the king in your house? Who makes the rules?

FRANK. Gentlemen ...

JOE. When Maggie wanted you to put in that new floor, you didn't bowl for two weeks, Charlie.

CHARLIE. Yeah, well that was different.

JOE. And because you couldn't bowl, you wouldn't let *us* bowl neither.

CHARLIE. Don't get small on me, okay?

JOE. Why was it so different —

CHARLIE. I hate it when you get *small* on me like that.

FRANK. Gentlemen, *please!* Peace. *(Joe and Charlie are quiet. After a moment.)*

JOE. And it's not doilies.

FRANK. Joe. Peace.

CHARLIE. Hey, how's your wife doin', Frankie?

FRANK. She's good.

CHARLIE. The doctor fix her all up and everything?

FRANK. Looks like it. She was out there mowing the grass yesterday.

CHARLIE. That's a sign.

FRANK. That's a sign. How 'bout that lawn mower you bought, Charlie? How's that working?

CHARLIE. Aaaaah, it's busted.

FRANK. Already?

CHARLIE. Yeah, it's busted.

FRANK. So take it back.

CHARLIE. Aaah, I don't know why I ever cut my grass in the first place. I *like* it long. I like to sit on my porch and look at it being long. Where do you think the word "lawn" comes from in the first place? From "long," because grass was always *long*. Originally people said I'm gonna plant some seeds and grow a long. Then some moron thought he'd be different, he cut his long short. The rest is the history of fashion.

FRANK. I didn't know that. *(Joe snickers loudly through his nose.)*
CHARLIE. You say something, Joe?
JOE. Who, me? I didn't say anything. *(A paper floats by. Charlie plucks it out of the air, glances at it cursorily, lets it float away again.)*
FRANK. *(Looks up and calls.)* Yo, Peptak! You got any sugar cubes? *(He holds out the cup of his thermos and a sugar cube drops into it from above.)* Thanks! *(An air mattress floats by. No comment from any of them.)*
CHARLIE. You guys ever think about hang-gliding home from here?
FRANK. Hang-gliding home?
CHARLIE. Yeah, instead of driving or taking the Path?
FRANK. Wouldn't you have to learn how to hang glide first?
CHARLIE. Well sure, you'd have to learn. But then after you wrapped up work you could strap on your wings, walk offa the top floor, and sail home. Be the first person in history to fly from 18th Street and Twelfth Avenue to Tenafly New Jersey. With a fabulous view all the way. Maybe after I retire …
FRANK. You know I been sitting here eating this thing, I still don't know if it's liverwurst or tuna?
CHARLIE. That's all the ozone up here. The carbon dioxide at this altitude compresses the things in your nose, you can't taste nothing. *(Joe snickers, louder than before.)* Did you say something, Joe?
JOE. Not me. I guess the carbon dioxide was compressing my nose or something.
FRANK. *(Glancing at the newspaper.)* Hey, speaking of flying, Charlie — they got that movie about the Lindbergh kid on tonight.
CHARLIE. They got the what?
FRANK. The Lindbergh baby who got kidnapped, they got the movie on again —
CHARLIE. Let me see that. Let me see that. *(He grabs the paper from Frank's hand.)*
FRANK. Hey, what's up? What the hell are you doing?
CHARLIE. Nothing. I just want to see. *(Reads intently.)* Uh-huh. Uh-huh …
FRANK. Did you see that movie that time it was on?

CHARLIE. Oh, yeah. I saw that movie.

FRANK. Anthony Hopkins, as what's-his-name ...

CHARLIE. Bruno Hauptmann.

FRANK. Hey didn't that happen someplace around — ?

CHARLIE. Hopewell, New Jersey.

JOE. What are they bringing that turkey back for?

CHARLIE. "Turkey?"

JOE. Yeah, who wants to see that turkey all over again?

CHARLIE. That is a very thoughtful movie, for your information. And as it happens today is the anniversary of the day that Charles Lindbergh's baby was kidnapped.

JOE. That happened 50 years ago! What's the big deal?

CHARLIE. Jesus Christ died on Easter, they show *The King of Kings* that weekend.

FRANK. Gentlemen ...

CHARLIE. And if you ever did anything more important than glue your wife's cat pictures into a photo album, they'd show "The Joe Morelli Story" on *your* birthday.

FRANK. Gentlemen, please!

CHARLIE. And don't let me hear the word "turkey."

FRANK. Hey what's with you today, Charlie? What's the matter?

CHARLIE. Nothing's the matter.

FRANK. You're acting all weird.

CHARLIE. I'm not weird.

FRANK. Okay.... Here, bird. Here, bird. Here, bird. *(He whistles to a passing bird, and tosses it a crumb. Charlie has taken a cupcake out of his lunch pail. He unobtrusively puts a candle in, and lights it.)* What the heck is *that?*

CHARLIE. What does it look like? It's a chocolate cupcake.

FRANK. Hey Joe, will you look at this?

JOE. Isn't that nice. Maggie made him a cupcake.

CHARLIE. My wife did not make me this cupcake, I *bought* this cupcake.

FRANK. But there's a candle in it.

CHARLIE. Yes. There is a candle in it.

FRANK. What's the celebration, Charlie?

CHARLIE. Who says there's a celebration?

FRANK. Corned beef and pastrami, now a chocolate cupcake?

CHARLIE. A somber color, if you will notice. Maybe I'm observing a very solemn day for some private reason.

JOE. Next thing you know he's going to be putting out doilies around his house.

CHARLIE. That's it, Morelli!

FRANK. Gentlemen —

JOE. And that Lindbergh movie is pedigree turkey.

CHARLIE. I TOLD YOU I DON'T WANT TO HEAR THE WORD "TURKEY!"

JOE. And if you ask me, Charles Lindbergh is overrated.

CHARLIE. Oh, he's overrated?

JOE. Yeah, overrated! So he flew across the —

CHARLIE. The greatest hero in American history?

JOE. He flew across the ocean, *big deal.*

CHARLIE. Oh big deal, huh?

JOE. Yeah. And as for the Lindbergh baby — who *cares?*

CHARLIE. Who cares?

JOE. Who the hell cares, it's old news!

CHARLIE. Well for your information —

JOE. Working people get kidnapped every day in the world, they don't make no movies about *them.*

CHARLIE. Maybe they're not as important as Charles Lindbergh Junior.

JOE. Why am I supposed to care about the goddamn Lindbergh baby?

CHARLIE. You don't care about the Lindbergh baby?

JOE. No, I don't care about the Lindbergh baby!

CHARLIE. You don't have any feeling for the Lindbergh baby?

JOE. No I don't have any feeling for the Lindbergh baby!

CHARLIE. For your information, *I AM the Lindbergh baby!* (*Long pause.*) Okay?

JOE. You're the...?

CHARLIE. *Yes.* I am the Lindbergh baby. I am the rightful son of Charles Lindbergh, kidnapped from the home of my parents on this very date, and I didn't mean to tell you but you forced me into it. And the hell if I will listen to my family be insulted! So there! *(Pause.)*

JOE.   You're the Lindb — ?

CHARLIE.   Yes.

FRANK.   But your name is Petrossian.

CHARLIE.   Oh sure. That's what I was brought up to *think* my name was.

JOE.   *YOU THINK YOU'RE THE LINDBERGH BABY?*

CHARLIE.   Go to hell, Joe.

JOE.   I don't believe this!

CHARLIE.   The truth is always a little strange at first sight. Okay?

JOE.   Do you know there are separate asylums to hold all the people who think they're the Lindbergh baby?

CHARLIE.   Yeah well those people are impostors, aren't they?

JOE.   I think you have gone offa your head!

CHARLIE.   Just mind your own business, will you? Stick to pickle and pimento loaf, Mr. Smalltime.

FRANK.   You know, Charlie, there *are* people who might — you know — wonder a little, if you claimed to be the Lindbergh baby.

CHARLIE.   But it all fits, don't it? I mean — "Charles Jr.?" "Charlie?" Was I not born in New Jersey in or around the significant date? Was I not brought up in the town of Hopewell, where the crime was perpetuated?

FRANK.   He *did* grow up in Hopewell, Joe.

JOE.   So did 20 million other babies.

FRANK.   I thought the police found the kid's body.

CHARLIE.   No, no, no. That was another kid's body.

FRANK.   Whose body?

CHARLIE.   I don't know whose body. But it certainly was not *my* body.

FRANK.   Sure, obviously not.

CHARLIE.   They never located me. You see? I'm still at large.

JOE.   I'll say you are.

FRANK.   How come you kept this a secret all these years, Charlie?

JOE.   Because people would think he was a fruitcake, that's why.

CHARLIE.   Naturally some people wouldn't believe me. Plus I was pretty well established as Charles Petrossian. You know — driver's license, credit cards, bank account ...

FRANK.   Sure, it's hard to make a change.

CHARLIE.   Mostly I didn't want to upset the feelings of my true mother, Anne Morrow Lindbergh.

JOE.   Whose books are bullshit.

CHARLIE.   You shut your trap about my mother!

JOE.   She made a goddamn fortune offa you, writing about that kidnapping. You oughta ask for a cut of the royalties. You could retire early, take up *hang gliding*.

CHARLIE.   I'm through talking to you.

FRANK.   Joe's got a point, Charlie. You ought to contact the Lindbergers.

CHARLIE.   Actually ... I did write to mother, once.

FRANK.   You did?

CHARLIE.   Yeah. I figure the letter never got to her.

FRANK.   Did you tell her — you know — who you were?

CHARLIE.   I *hinted* who I was.

JOE.   Oh sure. "Dear Mom. Please send the inheritance. Your loving son, Charles Petrossian."

CHARLIE.   Knock it off.

JOE.   Real subtle.

FRANK.   But this means Anthony Hopkins didn't kidnap you.

CHARLIE.   Not unless he was in league with the Petrossian family.

FRANK.   Ah-ha! What *about* the Petrossians' role in all this?

CHARLIE.   My foster parents, as I like to think of them? Pawns in a bigger game, Frankie. Pawns in a bigger game.

FRANK.   Well it's very funny you should be saying all this.

CHARLIE.   What, that I been the Lindbergh baby and you never knew it?

FRANK.   Yeah. Because you see — I'm the son of Czar Nicholas the Second of Russia.

CHARLIE.   No.

FRANK.   Yeah.

CHARLIE.   You're kidding.

FRANK.   It's the truth.

CHARLIE. The kid who got killed in the Russian Revolution?

FRANK. That's me. The heir to the throne of Moscow.

CHARLIE. Holy shit.

FRANK. And Sovereign of the Ukraine.

CHARLIE. I saw that movie! *Nicholas and What's-Her-Name.*

FRANK. Alexandra. That was *my* mother.

CHARLIE. But I thought you got shot.

FRANK. No. A faithful servant smuggled me out. Nobody knows I survived but me.

CHARLIE. And you had Sir Laurence Olivier in your movie.

FRANK. Yeah, I felt pretty honored, having Larry in my movie. Though I did have a few quibbles about the — you know — historical details.

CHARLIE. So what's your real name?

FRANK. Alexei Nikolaievitch Romanoff.

CHARLIE. By what name would you prefer to be called?

FRANK. Aaah, keep calling me Frank. It's easier.

JOE. THE CZAR OF RUSSIA?

CHARLIE. I don't want to hear a word from you.

JOE. THE CZAR OF RUSSIA? Do you know how old you'd have to be, to be the Czar of Russia?

CHARLIE. Never you mind, Frank.

JOE. You'd have to be 95 years old! And a hemophiliac!

FRANK. I've always been a heavy bleeder.

JOE. That don't make you the goddamn Czar of Russia!

CHARLIE. Will you just shut up, Joe? Please? You're on a lot of very sensitive ground. Frank here lost everybody in the Revolution. You're talking about family here. You're talking about orphans.

JOE. Okay then, "Alexei." How do you know you're the head honcho of the Ukraine?

FRANK. Well when I saw that movie, with the Kremlin, and those domes —

CHARLIE. The onion-shaped domes.

FRANK. The bunion-shaped domes, I said to myself, I've been there sometime! It was like I could remember it.

CHARLIE. Of course you'd remember it. Those Commie bastards tried to rub you out there. Was the movie a painful experience.?

FRANK. It only got bad when I had to watch myself get killed.

CHARLIE. Understandably, Alexei. Have you told Phyllis?

FRANK. No, not yet.

CHARLIE. She'll be pretty surprised to find out she's the Queen of Russia.

FRANK. Czarina.

CHARLIE. Huh?

FRANK. The wife of the Czar is the Czarina.

CHARLIE. Is that the proof, Joe? He's got the facts at the tips of his fingers.

JOE. I know how cars work, that don't make me an Oldsmobile.

FRANK. Peace, gentlemen. Peace.

CHARLIE. Just think. If we'd'a had you over there running things all these years, the Berlin Wall woulda gotten taken down a lot sooner than it did — after not being built in the *first* place.

FRANK. Yeah. It's tough, knowing what I could do for world peace.

CHARLIE. Well if things had worked out different, I can't think of anybody I'd rather have on the Russian throne than Frank Mikula.

FRANK. Thank you, Charlie.

CHARLIE. Well I'll be goddamned. To think all this time we never knew it. You didn't know about me. I didn't know about you. And Joe here didn't know about either one of us ...

FRANK. Yeah ... *(Silence. They turn and look at Joe.)* So, Joe ...

JOE. Yeah, what?

FRANK. Who are *you?*

JOE. I'm not anybody.

FRANK. No, really, I mean.

JOE. I'm not anybody. I'm Joe Morelli. Period.

FRANK. I'm not talking about that.

JOE. I'm Superman.

FRANK. Underneath it all.

JOE. Underneath it all I'm nobody. I'm just a guy on the street. Okay?

CHARLIE. Okay.

FRANK. Okay. *(Pause.)*

JOE. But in a previous lifetime, I was Marie Antoinette.

CHARLIE. No *shit!*

JOE. That was me!

FRANK. The let-'em-eat-cake lady?

JOE. I said that in 1793. "Let them eat cake!"

CHARLIE. Well isn't that something.

FRANK. I knew all along you were *some*body.

CHARLIE. Frank gets shot up by the Reds, you have your head chopped off in Par-ee.

JOE. Yeah. One minute I'm standing by a guillotine in a diamond tiara, next minute I'm Joe Morelli in Teaneck.

CHARLIE. Must be pretty disconcerting.

JOE. To say the least. *(Construction whistle, off.)*

CHARLIE. There's the whistle.

FRANK. Already?

CHARLIE. That's what the company says. On to the fifty-first story. *(They pack up their things.)*

JOE. But listen, you guys — I don't want this getting around. I mean, you can't tell nobody.

CHARLIE. We will be as the tomb.

JOE. You swear?

CHARLIE. Of course we swear.

FRANK. We're all in the same — you know —

ALL THREE. *(Together.)* Situation.

CHARLIE. Now first things first. Who is bowling tonight?

FRANK. I'm in.

CHARLIE. And I'm in. Joey?

JOE. I told you, Charlie. I got things I gotta do.

CHARLIE. Are you forgetting who you are? Your majesty?

FRANK. *Remember the crown jewels,* Joe.

JOE. You're right. Let's bowl. *(They cheer.)* And *c'est la guerre!*

CHARLIE and FRANK. *La guerre!*

JOE. Long as I'm home by midnight.

CHARLIE. What are you now — Cinderella? *(He sings.)* "I'm the man!"

FRANK and JOE. "He's the man!!"

CHARLIE. "I'm the man!"

FRANK and JOE. "He's the man!"

ALL THREE. "I'm the man who broke the bank at Monte Carlo!" *(A bird sails by.)*

BLACKOUT

PROPERTY LIST

Sandwiches (JOE, FRANK, CHARLIE)
Newspaper (JOE)
Lunch pails (CHARLIE, FRANK)
Paper
Thermos cup (FRANK)
Sugar cube
Air mattress
Cupcake (CHARLIE)
Candle (CHARLIE)
Matches or lighter (CHARLIE)

SOUND EFFECTS

Construction site whistle

TIME FLIES

this play is for
John Rando,
Anne O'Sullivan, Arnie Burton,
and Willis Sparks,
who made it fly

TIME FLIES was first produced at Primary Stages Company (Casey Childs, Artistic Director) in New York City, as part of the evening MERE MORTALS, in May, 1997. The play was directed by John Rando; the set design was by Russell Metheny; the costume design was by Anita Yavich; the lighting design was by Phil Monat; the sound design was by Aural Fixation; and the stage manager was Christine Catti. The cast was as follows:

MAY .... Anne O'Sullivan
HORACE .... Arnie Burton
DAVID ATTENBOROUGH .... Willis Sparks

TIME FLIES

Evening. A pond. Upstage, a thicket of tall cattails. Down-stage, a deep green love seat and a cricket coffee table. Over-head, an enormous full moon.

A loud cuckoo sounds, like the mechanical "CUCKOO" of a clock.

Lights come up on two mayflies, Horace and May, buzzing as they "fly" in. They are dressed like singles on an evening out, he in a jacket and tie, she in a fetching party dress — but they have insect-like antennae, long tube-like tails, and on their backs, translucent wings. Outsized hornrim glasses give the impression of very large eyes. May has distinctly hairy legs.

HORACE and MAY.   *Bzzzzzzzzzzzzzzzzz … (Their wings stop flut-tering, as they "settle.")*
MAY.   Well here we are. This is my place.
HORACE.   Already? That was fast.
MAY.   Swell party, huh.
HORACE.   Yeah. Quite a swarm.
MAY.   Thank you for flying me home.
HORACE.   No. Sure. I'm happy to. Absolutely. My pleasure. I mean — you're very, very, very welcome. *(Their eyes lock and they near each other as if for a kiss, their wings fluttering a little.)* Bzzzzzz …
MAY.   Bzzzzzzzz … *(Before their jaws can meet: we hear another "CUCKOO!" and Horace breaks away.)*
HORACE.   It's that late, is it. Anyway, it was very nice meet-ing you — I'm sorry, is it April?
MAY.   May.
HORACE.   May. Yes. Later than I thought, huh.

MAY.   That's very funny, Vergil.

HORACE.   It's Horace, actually.

MAY.   I'm sorry. The buzz at that party was so loud.

HORACE.   So you're "May the mayfly."

MAY.   Yeah. Guess my parents didn't have much imagination. May, mayfly.

HORACE.   You don't, ah, live with your parents, do you, May?

MAY.   No, my parents died around dawn this morning.

HORACE.   Isn't that funny. Mine died around dawn too.

MAY.   That *is* funny. Or maybe it's fate.

HORACE.   Is that what it izzzzzzzz...?

MAY.   Bzzzzzzzz ...

HORACE.   Bzzzzzzzzzzzzz ... *(They near for a kiss, but Horace breaks away.)* Well I'd better be going now. Good night. *(He starts out.)*

MAY.   Would you like a drink? *(Horace comes back.)*

HORACE.   I'd love a drink, actually ...

MAY.   Let me just turn on a couple of fireflies. *(May tickles the underside of a couple of two-foot long fireflies hanging like a chandelier, and they light up.)*

HORACE.   Wow. Great *pond!* *(Indicating the love seat.)* I love the lily pad.

MAY.   That was here. It kinda grew on me. Care to take the load off your wings?

HORACE.   That's all right. I'll just — you know — hover. But will you look at that...! *(Turning to look at the cricket coffee table, Horace bats May with his wings.)*

MAY.   Oof!

HORACE.   I'm sorry. Did we collide?

MAY.   No. No. It's fine.

HORACE.   I've only had my wings about six hours ...

MAY.   Really? So have I...!

HORACE.   Isn't that funny.

MAY.   Wasn't molting *disgusting?*

HORACE.   Eugh. I'm glad *that's* over.

MAY.   Care for some music? I've got The Beatles, The Byrds, The Crickets ...

HORACE.   I love the Crickets.

MAY.   Well so do I ... *(She kicks the coffee table, and we hear the buzz of crickets. They boogie to the sound of the crickets.)*

HORACE.   So are you going out with any — I mean, are there any other mayflies in the neighborhood?

MAY.   No, it's mostly wasps.

HORACE.   So, you live here by your, um, all by yourself? Alone?

MAY.   All by my lonesome.

HORACE.   And will you look at that moon.

MAY.   You know that's the first moon I've ever seen?

HORACE.   That's the first moon *I've* ever seen...!

MAY.   Isn't that funny.

HORACE.   When were you born?

MAY.   About 7:30 this morning.

HORACE.   So was I! Seven thirty-three!

MAY.   Isn't that funny.

HORACE.   Or maybe it's fate. *(They near each other again, as if for a kiss.)* Bzzzzzzz ...

MAY.   Bzzzzzzzzz ... I think that moon is having a very emotional effect on me.

HORACE.   Me too.

MAY.   It must be nature.

HORACE.   Me too.

MAY.   Or maybe it's fate.

HORACE.   Me too ...

A FROG.   *(Amplified, over loudspeaker.) RIBBIT, RIBBIT!*

HORACE.   A frog!

MAY.   A frog!

HORACE and MAY.   *The frogs are coming, the frogs are coming! (They "fly" around the stage in a panic. Ad lib.) A frog, a frog! The frogs are coming, the frogs are coming! (They finally stop, breathless.)*

MAY.   It's okay. It's okay.

HORACE.   Oh my goodness.

MAY.   I think he's gone now.

HORACE.   Oh my goodness, that scared me.

MAY.   That is the only drawback to living here. The frogs.

HORACE. You know I like frog films and frog literature. I just don't like frogs.

MAY. And they're so rude if you're not a frog yourself.

HORACE. Look at me. I'm still shaking.

MAY. Why don't I fix you something. Would you like a grass-hopper? Or a stinger?

HORACE. Just some stagnant water would be fine.

MAY. A little duckweed in that? Some algae?

HORACE. Straight up is fine.

MAY. Sure I couldn't tempt you to try the lily pad?

HORACE. Well, maybe for just a second. *(Horace flutters down onto the love seat.)* Zzzzzz …

MAY. *(Handing him a glass.)* Here you go. Cheers, Horace.

HORACE. Long life, May. *(They clink glasses.)*

MAY. Do you want to watch some tube?

HORACE. Some tube. Sure. What's on?

MAY. Let's see. *(She checks a green TV guide.)* There is … *The Love Bug. M. Butterfly. The Spider's Stratagem. Travels With My Ant. Angels and Insects. The Fly* …

HORACE. The original, or Jeff Goldblum?

MAY. Jeff Goldblum.

HORACE. Euch. Too gruesome.

MAY. *Born Yesterday.* And *Life On Earth.*

HORACE. What's on that?

MAY. "Swamp Life," with Sir David Attenborough.

HORACE. That sounds good.

MAY. Shall we try it?

HORACE. Carpe diem.

MAY. Carpe diem? What's that?

HORACE. I don't know. It's Latin.

MAY. What's Latin?

HORACE. I don't know. I'm just a mayfly. *("CUCKOO!")* And we're right on time for it. *(May presses a remote control and at stage left David Attenborough appears, wearing a safari jacket.)*

DAVID ATTENBOROUGH. Hello, I'm David Attenborough. Welcome to "Swamp Life."

MAY. Isn't this comfy.

HORACE. Is my wing in your way?

54

MAY.   No. It's fine.

DAVID ATTENBOROUGH.   You may not believe it, but within this seemingly lifeless puddle, there thrives a teeming world of vibrant life.

HORACE.   May, look! Isn't that *your* pond?

MAY.   I think that is my pond!

HORACE.   He said "puddle."

DAVID ATTENBOROUGH.   This puddle is only several inches across, but its stagnant water plays host to over 14 *gazillion* different species.

MAY.   It is my pond!

DAVID ATTENBOROUGH.   Every species here is engaged in a constant, desperate battle for survival. Feeding — meeting — mating — breeding — dying. And mating. And meeting. And mating. And feeding. And dying. Mating. Mating. Meeting. Breeding. Brooding. Braiding — those that can braid. Feeding. Mating.

MAY.   All *right,* Sir Dave!

DAVID ATTENBOROUGH.   Mating, mating, and mating.

HORACE.   Only one thing on *his* mind.

MAY.   The filth on television these days.

DAVID ATTENBOROUGH.   Tonight we start off with one of the saddest creatures of this environment.

HORACE.   The dung beetle.

MAY.   The toad.

DAVID ATTENBOROUGH.   The lowly mayfly.

HORACE.   Did he say "the mayfly"?

MAY.   I think he said the *lowly* mayfly.

DAVID ATTENBOROUGH.   Yes. The lowly mayfly. Like these two mayflies, for instance.

HORACE.   May — I think that's us!

MAY.   Oh my God …

HORACE and MAY.   *(Together.) We're on television!*

HORACE.   I don't believe it!

MAY.   Oh, I wish my mother was here to see this!

HORACE.   This is amazing!

MAY.   Oh God, I look terrible!

HORACE.   You look very good.

MAY.   I can't look at this.

DAVID ATTENBOROUGH.   As you see, the lowly mayfly is not one of nature's most attractive creatures.

MAY.   Well at least we don't wear safari jackets.

HORACE.   I wish he'd stop saying "*lowly* mayfly."

DAVID ATTENBOROUGH.   The lowly mayfly has a very distinctive *khkhkhkhkhkhkhkhkhkkh* ... (*The sound of TV "static."*)

MAY.   I think there's something wrong with my antenna ... *(She adjusts the antenna on her head.)*

HORACE.   You don't have cable?

MAY.   Not on this pond.

DAVID ATTENBOROUGH.   *(Stops the static sound.)* ... and sixty tons of droppings.

HORACE.   There. That fixed it.

MAY.   Can I offer you some food? I've got some plankton in the pond. And some very nice gnat.

HORACE.   I do love good gnat.

MAY.   I'll set it out, you can pick.

DAVID ATTENBOROUGH.   The lowly mayfly first appeared some 350 million years ago ...

MAY.   That's impressive.

DAVID ATTENBOROUGH.   ... and is of the order Ephemeroptera, meaning, "living for a single day."

MAY.   I did not know that!

HORACE.   "Living for a single day." Huh ...

MAY.   *(Setting out a tray on the coffee table.)* There you go.

HORACE.   Gosh, May. That's beautiful.

MAY.   There's curried gnat, salted gnat, Scottish smoked gnat ...

HORACE.   I love that.

MAY.   ... gnat with pesto, gnat au naturelle, and Gnat King Cole.

HORACE.   I don't think I could finish a whole one.

MAY.   "Gnat" to worry. *(They laugh politely.)* That's larva dip there in the center. Just dig in.

DAVID ATTENBOROUGH.   As for the life of the common mayfly ...

HORACE.   Oh. We're "common" now.

DAVID ATTENBOROUGH.   ... it is a simple round of meeting, mating, meeting, mating —

MAY.   Here we go again.

DAVID ATTENBOROUGH.   — breeding, feeding, feeding ...

HORACE.   This dip is fabulous.

DAVID ATTENBOROUGH.   ... and dying.

MAY.   Leaf?

HORACE.   Thank you. *(May breaks a leaf off a plant and hands it to Horace to use as a napkin.)*

DAVID ATTENBOROUGH.   Mayflies are a major food source for trout and salmon. *(He produces a large fish from his pocket.)*

HORACE and MAY.   Eugh! Ugh!

MAY.   Will you look at that?

HORACE.   Revolting.

DAVID ATTENBOROUGH.   Fishermen like to bait hooks with mayfly lookalikes.

MAY.   *Bastards.* Excuse me.

DAVID ATTENBOROUGH.   And then there is the giant bullfrog.

A FROG.   *(Amplified, over loudspeaker.) RIBBIT, RIBBIT!*

HORACE and MAY.   *The frogs are coming, the frogs are coming! (They "fly" around the stage in a panic — and end up "flying" right into each other's arms.)*

HORACE.   Well there.

MAY.   Hello.

DAVID ATTENBOROUGH.   Welcome to "Swamp Life!" *(David Attenborough exits.)*

MAY.   Funny how we flew right into each other's wings.

HORACE.   It is funny.

MAY.   Or fate.

HORACE.   Do you think he's gone?

MAY.   David Attenborough?

HORACE.   The frog.

MAY.   What frog. Bzzzz ...

HORACE.   Bzzzzz ... *(With their hands, they rub each other's noses.)*

DAVID ATTENBOROUGH'S VOICE.   As you see, mayflies can be quite affectionate, mutually palpating their proboscises.

HORACE. You know I've been wanting to palpate your proboscis all evening?

MAY. I think it was larva at first sight.

HORACE and MAY. *(Rubbing proboscises together.)* Zzzzzzzzzzzzz-zzzzzzzzzzzz ...

MAY. *(Very "Brief Encounter" British.)* Oh darling, darling.

HORACE. Oh do darling do let's always be good to each other, shall we?

MAY. Let's do do that, darling, always, always.

HORACE. Always?

MAY. Always.

HORACE and MAY. *Zzzzzzzzzzzzzzzzzzzzzzzzzzzz!*

MAY. Rub my antennae. Rub my antennae. *(Horace rubs May's antennae with his hands.)*

DAVID ATTENBOROUGH'S VOICE. Sometimes mayflies rub antennae together.

MAY. Oh yes. Yes. Just like that. Yes. Keep going. Harder. Rub harder.

HORACE. Rub mine now. Rub my antennae. Oh yes. Yes. Yes. Yes. There's the rub. There's the rub. Go. Go. Go!

DAVID ATTENBOROUGH'S VOICE. Isn't that a picture. Now get a load of mating. *(Horace gets into mounting position behind May. He rubs her antennae while she wolfs down the gnat-food in front of her.)*

HORACE and MAY. *BZZZZZZZZZZZZZZZZZZZZZZZZZZZZZ-ZZZZZZZZZZZZZZZZZZZZZZZZZZZZZZZ!*

DAVID ATTENBOROUGH'S VOICE. Unfortunately for this insect, the mayfly has a lifespan of only one day. *(Horace and May stop buzzing, abruptly.)*

HORACE. What was that...?

DAVID ATTENBOROUGH'S VOICE. The mayfly has a lifespan of only one day — living just long enough to meet, mate, have offspring, and die.

MAY. Did he say "meet, mate, have offspring, and *DIE*" — ?

DAVID ATTENBOROUGH'S VOICE. I did. In fact, mayflies born at 7:30 in the morning will die by the next dawn. *(Horace whimpers at the thought.)* But so much for the lowly mayfly. Let's move on to the newt. *("CUCKOO!")*

HORACE.   We're going to die…!

MAY.   We're going to die…!

HORACE and MAY.   *Mayday, mayday! We're going to die, we're going to die! (Weeping and wailing.)* Wah-ha-ha-ha! *(Still wailing, they kneel, beat their breasts, cross themselves, daven, and tear their hair. Till: "CUCKOO!")*

HORACE.   What time is it? What time is it?

MAY.   I don't wear a watch. I'm a lowly *mayfly!*

HORACE.   *(Gasping for breath.)* Oh my goodness. I think I'm having an asthma attack. Can mayflies have asthma?

MAY.   I don't know. Ask Mr. Safari Jacket.

HORACE.   Maybe if I put a paper bag over my head …

MAY.   So this is my sex life?

HORACE.   Do you have a paper bag?

MAY.   One bang, a bambino, and boom — that's it?

HORACE.   Do you have a paper bag?

MAY.   For the common mayfly, foreplay segues right into funeral.

HORACE.   Do you have a paper bag?

MAY.   I don't have time to look for a paper bag, I'm going to be *dead* very shortly, all right? *("CUCKOO!")*

HORACE.   Oh come on! That wasn't a whole hour! *("CUCKOO!")* Time is moving so fast now. *("CUCKOO!")*

HORACE and MAY.   SHUT UP! *("CUCKOO!")* Wah-ha-ha-ha …

HORACE.   *(Suddenly sober.)* Well this explains everything. We were born this morning, we hit puberty in mid-afternoon, our biological clocks went "bong," and here we are. Hot to copulate.

MAY.   For the one brief miserable time we get to do it.

HORACE.   Yeah.

MAY.   Talk about a quickie.

HORACE.   Wait a minute, wait a minute.

MAY.   Talk fast.

HORACE.   What makes you think it would be so *brief?*

MAY.   Oh, I'm sorry. Did I insult your vast sexual experience?

HORACE.   Are you more experienced than *I* am, Dr. Ruth? Luring me here to your pad?

MAY. I see. I see. Blame me!

HORACE. Can I remind you we only get one shot at this?

MAY. So I can rule out multiple orgasms, is that it?

HORACE. I'm just saying there's not a lot of time to hone one's erotic technique, okay?

MAY. Hmp!

HORACE. And I'm trying to sort out some very big ento-montological questions here rather *quickly,* do you mind?

MAY. And I'm just the babe here, is that it? I'm just a piece of tail?

HORACE. I'm not the one who suggested TV.

MAY. I'm not the one who wanted to watch *Life On Earth.* "Oh, 'Swamp Life.' That sounds *interesting.*"

A FROG. *RIBBIT, RIBBIT.*

HORACE. *(Calmly.)* There's a frog up there.

MAY. Oh, I'm really scared. I'm terrified.

A FROG. *RIBBIT, RIBBIT!*

HORACE. *(Calling to the frog.)* We're right down here! Come and get us!

MAY. Breeding. Dying. Breeding. Dying. So this is the whole purpose of mayflies? To make more mayflies?

HORACE. Does the world *need* more mayflies?

MAY. We're a major food source for trout and salmon.

HORACE. How nice for the salmon.

MAY. Do you want more food?

HORACE. I've lost a bit of my appetite, all right?

MAY. Oh. Excuse me.

HORACE. I'm sorry. Really, May.

MAY. You think I don't feel bad? *Males!*

HORACE. Leaf? *(He plucks another leaf and hands it to her.)*

MAY. Thank you. *(She blows her nose into the leaf.)*

HORACE. Really. I didn't mean to snap at you.

MAY. Oh, you've been very nice. *("CUCKOO!" They jump.)* Under the circumstances.

HORACE. I'm sorry.

MAY. No, I'm sorry.

HORACE. No, I'm sorry.

MAY. No, I'm sorry.

HORACE.   No, I'm sorry.

MAY.   We'd better stop apologizing, we're going to be dead soon.

HORACE.   I'm sorry.

MAY.   Oh Horace, I had such plans. I had such wonderful plans. I wanted to see Paris.

HORACE.   What's Paris?

MAY.   I have no fucking idea.

HORACE.   Maybe we'll come back as caviar and find out. *(They laugh a little at that.)* I was just hoping to live till Tuesday.

MAY.   What's a Tuesday? *(They laugh a little more at that.)* The sun's going to be up soon. I'm scared, Horace. I'm so scared.

HORACE.   You know, May, we don't have much time, and really, we hardly know each other — but I'm going to say it. I think you're swell. I think you're divine. From your buggy eyes to the thick raspy hair on your legs to the intoxicating scent of your secretions.

MAY.   Eeeuw.

HORACE.   Eeeuw? No. I say *woof.* And I say who cares if life is a swamp and we're just a couple of small bugs in a very small pond. I say live, May! I say — darn it — live!

MAY.   But how?

HORACE.   Well I don't honestly know ...

DAVID ATTENBOROUGH'S VOICE.   You could fly to Paris.

MAY.   We could fly to Paris!

HORACE.   Do we have time to fly to Paris?

MAY.   Carpe diem!

HORACE.   What is carpe diem?

DAVID ATTENBOROUGH'S VOICE.   It means *"bon voyage."*

HORACE.   *(Holding out a hand.)* Ignition.

MAY.   *(Taking his hand.)* Contact.

HORACE and MAY.   And we're outa here! *(They fly off to Paris as the lights black out.)*

PROPERTY LIST

Drinking glasses (MAY)
Green TV guide (MAY)
Remote control (MAY)
Tray (MAY)
Plant leaf (MAY, HORACE)
Large fish (DAVID ATTENBOROUGH)

SOUND EFFECTS

Cuckoo clock
Crickets
Frog sounds

MERE MORTALS

ACT TWO

SPEED-THE-PLAY

Revised Edition

this play is for
Martha,
because it made her laugh
and just because

SPEED-THE-PLAY was originally presented in somewhat different form at the Mitzi Newhouse Theatre of Lincoln Center (Gregory Mosher, Artistic Director) in New York City, in November, 1989, as part of a Broadway Cares benefit honoring David Mamet. The director was Gregory Mosher and the cast was as follows:

M.C. .... Roderick McLachlan

American Buffalo
DON .... J.J. Johnston
BOBBY.. W.H. Macy
TEACH .... Mike Nussbaum

Speed-the-Plow
GOULD .... Joe Mantegna
FOX .... Bob Balaban
KAREN .... Felicity Huffman

Sexual Perversity in Chicago
BERNIE .... Treat Williams
DANNY.. Steven Goldstein
DEBORAH .... Mariel Hemingway
JOAN .... Felicity Huffman

Glengarry Glen Ross
LEVENE .... Robert Prosky
WILLIAMSON .... W.H. Macy
MOSS.. J.J. Johnston
AARONOW .... Mike Nussbaum
ROMA .... Joe Mantegna
CUSTOMER .... Steven Goldstein

SPEED-THE-PLAY

A meeting hall. A lectern. A banner that says "CHICAGO ILL MENS CLUB." A row of five old folding chairs and a card table with a telephone on it. Upstage, on the back wall, a large ceremonial portrait of David Mamet smoking a cigar.

At right, in the chairs, talking among themselves, are three men dressed in blue-collar gear, smoking cigars and drinking beer. At left are two women, dressed as blue-collar babes.

The M.C. is at the lectern. The M.C. is a man — but he is played by a woman in Mamet gear: a jacket, a baseball cap, and glasses. She carries a large phallic cigar.

M.C.   David. Mamet. Poker player. Cigar smoker. Male bonder. Winner of the Pulitzer Prize. Film director. Chicagoan. *Genius. (Sounds of approval from the men.)* Why is David Mamet an American genius? Because David Mamet instinctively knows three important things about his audience. First — he knows Americans like speed. Things that are fast. This is, after all, the country that invented the rock song ...

MEN.   Yeah!

M.C.   The roller coaster ...

MEN.   Yeah!

M.C.   And premature ejaculation.

MEN.   Yeah! Huh...?

M.C.   Okay, so we didn't invent premature ejaculation. Well we fucking *could* have. If we had thought of it. And we perfected it.

BABES.   Yeah!

M.C.   So anyway, Mamet keeps his plays in fifth gear. Second — David Mamet knows that Americans don't like to pay for parking. They also don't give a shit about theatre. Forty-seven-fifty plus dinner to listen to some pansy stand on a stage and *talk?* FUCK. THAT. So he keeps his plays nice and short. Third — David Mamet knows how Americans talk. Especially American men. He knows that when men go to the theatre, they want to hear familiar words like "asshole," and "jagoff." This is a.) liberating for our fucked-up puritanical bourgeois culture, b.) puts the mirror up to bullshit, and c.) directs our national attention where it oughta be. *(Adjusts her crotch.)* On *men.* David Mamet is the William Congreve of our time, and if you don't know who William Congreve is, you can suck — my — dick. We are gathered here tonight to honor Mr. Mamet for his contribution to the American theatre. For those of you who might not be familiar with the Master's work, I have boiled down a few of the major plays and summarized the gist, so to speak, to give you the Master's *oovruh* in the Master's own way: short, and to the fuckin' *point.* Four plays in seven minutes. Prepare to enter ... the Mamet Zone. *(She rings a fight bell.) American Buffalo.* Act One. A junk shop. *(Don and Bobby enter.)*

DON.   Bobby, you're a young punk.

BOBBY.   Fuckin' right I am.

DON.   A small-time thief.

BOBBY.   Fuckin' right I am.

DON.   But we never use the word "thief" do we, Bobby?

BOBBY.   Fuckin' right we don't.

DON.   And do you fence stolen goods through my junk shop?

BOBBY.   We never talk about it.

DON.   You're fuckin' right we don't.

BOBBY.   So what do we talk about, Donny?

DON.   The nature of life. We also say "fuck" a lot. *(Teach enters.)*

TEACH.   Fuckin' *life.*

DON.   Teach! Is it bad?

TEACH.   It's very bad.

DON.   Go for coffee, Bob. *(Bobby exits.)*

TEACH.   Fuckin' Fletcher. Fuckin' Ruthie.

DON.   So you seen Ruthie heretofore?

TEACH.   I'm over in the coffee shop puttin' my finger on the Zeitgeist, Ruthie starts talkin' objective correlatives. Next thing I know, form follows content, this fuckin' bitch goes traveling around the corner with my *sweet* roll, for which I paid for, sixty-fi' cents plus a ton of stolen pig-iron. As for fuckin' I-don't-give-a-shit-what-anybody-says *Fletcher,* I say the guy is a hair-dresser, and I only hope some vicious lesbo with a zipgun rips his fuckin' lips off, sends 'em in to Boys' Life magazine, and prints 'em up in a two-page spread that says "Oh Shit" to all eternity. What's new?

DON.   Not much. Maybe I'll ask Bobby to steal some buffalo-head nickels tonight.

TEACH.   Why?

DON.   To illustrate the nature of American capitalism.

TEACH.   Oh. Why don't I steal 'em instead?

DON.   Okay. *(Bell.)*

M.C.   Act Two. That night.

TEACH.   Everything's fucked up, Donny. I can't steal the coins.

DON.   I fear I detect a rationalization, Teach.

TEACH.   Why don't you go take a leak in the gene pool you swam in on. *(Bobby enters.)*

BOBBY.   Hey, Donny. Wanna buy this rare buffalo-head nickel?

TEACH.   Fuck you, Bobby.

DON.   Fuck you, Teach.

TEACH.   Fuck you, Donny.

BOBBY.   Fuck you, Donny and Teach.

TEACH.   Is there anybody who hasn't said fuck yet? *(They shake their heads "no.")* Then I guess that says it. *(Three bells.)*

M.C.   Yes, that says it. The cry of a man trapped in a man's body, in one Anglo-Saxon syllable ...

M.C. and MEN.   *Fuck! (Bell.)*

M.C.   We jump to an opus from the Master's late period, an example of his complex, Harry Jamesian style. *(Bell.) Oleanna* — whatever the fuck *that* means — Act One. A professor's office. *(John and Carol enter.)*

JOHN.   So you …

CAROL.   I. I. I …

JOHN.   But.

CAROL.   When the …

JOHN.   *No. No. No.* You do *not. (Phone rings. Into phone.)* House! Get me house! I want HOUSE, baby! *(Hangs up.)*

CAROL.   I. I. I …

JOHN.   Me teacher. You student.

CAROL.   No, but —

JOHN.   An effort to communi —

CAROL.   I. I. I …

JOHN.   An effort to *communicate* —

CAROL.   I SO STUPID! *(Phone rings.)*

JOHN,   *(Into phone.)* HOUSE! Get me HOUSE! *(Hangs up.)*

CAROL.   But in your class, you —

JOHN.   Me like you.

CAROL.   But in your class you said —

JOHN.   No. No. No. I may have *spoken,* but I did not *say* …

CAROL.   *(Weeping.)* I NO UNDERSTAND!

JOHN.   I'll give you an "A."

CAROL.   You will?

JOHN.   Now get the fuck outa here. *(Bell.)*

M.C.   Act Two. More of same.

CAROL.   You molested me.

JOHN.   Didn't.

CAROL.   Did.

JOHN.   Didn't.

CAROL.   Did.

JOHN.   Didn't.

CAROL.   Did. *(Three bells.)*

M.C.   I think that says it. She's wrong, he's right.

CAROL.   Wait a minute, wait a minute …

M.C.   Yeah, wait on this. We move on to *Speed The Plow* — Act One. An office in Hollywood. *(Bell. Fox and Gould enter.)*

FOX.   Gould, you are the new head of production at this studio.

GOULD.   I am.

FOX.   I am an unsuccessful independent producer.

GOULD. You are.

FOX. And you owe me a favor.

GOULD. Forsooth?

FOX. I own this piece-a-shit movie script. Will you take it to the head of the studio and make me rich?

GOULD. I'll do it at ten o'clock tomorrow morning.

FOX. Thank you, Gould.

GOULD. I'm a whore.

FOX. I'm a whore too.

GOULD. And we're *men*.

FOX. Who's your sexy new secretary?

GOULD. Some fuckin' temp.

FOX. I bet you 500 bills you can't get her in the sack.

GOULD. It's a bet. *(Into intercom.)* Karen, would you come in here, please? *(Karen enters.)*

KAREN. Sir?

GOULD. Karen, would you read this book about cosmic bullshit and come to my house tonight to report on it?

KAREN. Yes sir. *(Karen exits.)*

GOULD. Consider her fucked. *(Bell. Fox exits.)*

M.C. Act Two. Gould's house, that evening. *(Gould and Karen.)*

GOULD. Did you read the book about cosmic bullshit, Karen?

KAREN. Yes and I think the book is brilliant.

GOULD. It might be.

KAREN. And Mr. Fox's script is trash.

GOULD. It may be.

KAREN. So why will you produce it?

GOULD. Because I'm a whore.

KAREN. *I* think you're a very sensitive man.

GOULD. At last a girl who understands me! *(They embrace. Bell. Karen exits.)*

M.C. Act Three. Gould's office, the next morning. *(Gould and Fox.)*

GOULD. I'm not gonna recommend your script, Fox.

FOX. No?

GOULD. I'm not going to the head of the studio with it.

FOX. No?

GOULD. I'm gonna recommend this brilliant book on cosmic bullshit. Why? Because the business of America is Byzantine.

FOX. You lift your leg to pee.

GOULD. You genuflect to pick your nose.

FOX. You stand on your head to jerk off.

GOULD. You bounce on a trampoline to defecate.

FOX. You're only doing this because that *shtupka* went to bed with you and fired off a 2l-gun salute on your weenie. *(Small pause.)*

GOULD. You're right. *(Into intercom.)* Karen, would you come in here, please? *(Karen enters.)*

KAREN. Bob. Bob. Bob ...

GOULD. You're fired. *(Karen exits.)*

FOX. She's a whore.

GOULD. She's a whore.

FOX. And you're my friend.

GOULD. If only we were women, we could be lesbians together. *(Three bells.)*

M.C. Now there are those polymorphously pre-verse critics who say that Mr. Mamet's attitude toward women is somewhat shall we say "retrograde"? But may I point out that a good number of these carping critics are they themselves *women?* Creatures who are physically incapable of peeing against a tree trunk without wetting their nylons? 'Nuff said? Bite. Me. And to prove my point — if point I have one — an early romantic work. *(Bell.)* *Sexual Perversity in Chicago.* Scene One. A singles bar. *(Danny and Bernie enter.)*

BERNIE. All women are alike, Danny.

DANNY. Gosh, Bernie. Is that really true?

BERNIE. Essentially they're bitches.

DANNY. Or else they're whores?

BERNIE. Yes. Or else they're whores. *(Bell.)*

M.C. Scene Two. Joan and Deborah's apartment. *(Joan and Deborah enter.)*

JOAN. All men are alike, Deborah.

DEBORAH. They certainly are, Joan.

JOAN and DEBORAH. They're *men.* *(Bell.)*

M.C. Scene Three. A singles bar. *(Joan, alone. Bernie enters.)*

BERNIE. Hi there.

JOAN. Get lost.

BERNIE. You got a lotta fuckin' *nerve. (Bell.)*

M.C. Scene Four. A library. *(Deborah, alone. Danny enters.)*

DANNY. Hi there.

DEBORAH. Get lost.

DANNY. Want to go out with me?

DEBORAH. Okay. *(Bell.)*

M.C. Round Five. Bernie's apartment. *(Bernie, alone.)*

BERNIE. Is there a metaphysical point to broads? *(Bell.)*

M.C. Scene Six. Danny's apartment. *(Danny and Deborah in bed.)*

DANNY. Breast.

DEBORAH. Sperm.

DANNY. Penis.

DEBORAH. Menstruation.

DANNY. Masturbation.

DEBORAH. Your come smells just like Clorox.

DANNY. I think I'm falling in love with you.

M.C. He does so. The *fool. (Bell.)* Scene Seven. A bar. *(Danny, Deborah and Bernie.)*

DANNY. *(Introducing.)* Bernie, Deborah. Deborah, Bernie.

DEBORAH and BERNIE. Hello!

BERNIE. You sure are a nice girl, Deborah. *(Aside to Danny.)* Probably a whore. *(Bell.)*

M.C. Scene Eight. Deborah and Joan's apartment. *(Joan and Deborah.)*

JOAN. Is there a metaphysical point to men? *(Deborah is about to answer but … the bell rings. As she exits.)* Jesus Christ …

M.C. Scene Nine. A toy shop. *(Danny and Bernie enter.)*

BERNIE. When I was a child, an old man once placed his hand upon my genitals in a movie theatre.

DANNY. Upon your genitals?

BERNIE. In a movie theatre.

DANNY. Was it psychologically damaging?

BERNIE. How do I know, Danny? I was only a fucking *child. (Bell.)*

M.C. Scene Ten. A restaurant. *(Deborah and Joan enter.)*

DEBORAH. I'm going to move in with Danny. *(Joan puts her finger down her throat and gags. Bell.)*

M.C. Scene Eleven. The office. *(Danny and Bernie enter.)*

BERNIE. Ba-da *deep*, ba-da *dop*, ba-da *doop*, Dan.

DANNY. I know that, Bernie.

BERNIE. Da-da-daaa some girl, da-da-daaa it's love, da-da-daaa you're fucked.

DANNY. I see your point.

BERNIE. Oop scoop a wee-bop, bonk, *deek!*

DANNY. Yep. *(Bell.)*

M.C. Scene Twelve. Danny and Deborah's apartment. *(Danny and Deborah enter.)*

DEBORAH. Will you still love me when I'm old?

DANNY. Bitch.

DEBORAH. Jerk. I'm moving out. *(Bell.)*

M.C. Scene Thirteen. Joan and Deborah's apartment. *(Joan and Deborah enter.)*

JOAN. All men are alike, Deborah.

DEBORAH. Oh shut the fuck up. *(Bell.)*

M.C. Scene Fourteen. A beach.

DANNY. All women are alike, Bernie.

BERNIE. Gosh, Danny. Is that really true?

DANNY. Essentially they're bitches.

BERNIE. Or else they're whores?

DANNY. Or else they're whores. You want to go out with me?

BERNIE. Okay. *(Bell.)*

M.C. So there's the Master. Be with us next week for the complete works of Jean-Claude Van Damme.

BLACKOUT

PROPERTY LIST

Cigars (M.C., MEN)
Beer (MEN)

SOUND EFFECTS

Fight bell

DR. FRITZ
Or: The Forces of Light

this play was written for
and is dedicated to
the incomparable Nancy Opel

DR. FRITZ: OR THE FORCES OF LIGHT was first produced at Primary Stages Company (Casey Childs, Artistic Director) in New York City, as part of the evening MERE MORTALS, in May, 1997. The play was directed by John Rando; the set design was by Russell Metheny; the costume design was by Anita Yavich; the lighting design was by Phil Monat; the sound design was by Aural Fixation; and the stage manager was Christine Catti. The cast was as follows:

MARIA/DR. FRITZ... Nancy Opel
TOM .... Arnie Burton

DR. FRITZ
Or: The Forces of Light

Maria is sitting behind a crude plank table made from an old door. She wears a plain white linen smock and huaraches. She is knitting — but without any yarn.

On the table is a raggedy home-made doll with outstretched arms. Over the room hangs a rusty meathook. Upstage: a picture of Jesus as the Sacred Heart.

MARIA.   *(Sings, softly, calmly.) Corazona, corazona di Cristu! Wer bist Du? Wer bist Du? (Tom enters, holding his side and gasping in pain. He is dressed in Bermuda shorts, expensive sandals and a loud Hawaiian shirt.)*

TOM.   *Eugh. Eugh. Eugh.*

MARIA.   *Bendio, sinhors! Comari <u>ta</u>?*

TOM.   *Eugh?*

MARIA.   How you are feeling todays?

TOM.   *Eugh.*

MARIA.   *(Holds up the doll.)* You want to buy a souvenirs?

TOM.   *Eugh.*

MARIA.   One of a kinds.

TOM.   I'm looking for Dr. Fritz.

MARIA.   Ah, Dr. Fritz can cure everything. You have a troothache?

TOM.   No. Poison.

MARIA.   You have been poisoned? Tsk, tsk, tsk, tsk.

TOM.   Food poisoning.

MARIA.   Oh, the food poisonings. But no troothache?

TOM.   *I don't have a goddamn toothache.*

MARIA.   Eh, eh, eh. This is not nice languages, Pablo.

TOM.   Pablo?

MARIA.   I was foretold of a man named Pablo coming with a troothache.

TOM.   I'm not Pablo.

MARIA.   This is why you have no troothache.

TOM.   Look ...

MARIA.   *(Looking behind herself.)* Where?

TOM.   Listen ...

MARIA.   I hear nothings.

TOM.   My name is Tom Sanders. I'm staying at the Hotel Gorgon.

MARIA.   That's so nice.

TOM.   At the hotel I talked to this man Pedro ...

MARIA.   Pedro the doorman or Pedro the cook?

TOM.   Pedro the cook.

MARIA.   He so nice. You want to buy a souvenirs?

TOM.   No, thank you.

MARIA.   One of a kinds.

TOM.   Pedro said come here and ask for Dr. Fritz.

MARIA.   Ah, Dr. Fritz can cure everything. Broken bone, bullet hole, burn, amputation, housemaid's knee ...

TOM.   But —

MARIA.   Terminal diseases is more difficult.

TOM.   But —

MARIA.   This is why they are called terminal.

TOM.   But —

MARIA.   Ah, but are they terminal? A case for Dr. Fritz.

TOM.   But — doesn't the sign outside say "butcher"?

MARIA.   You speak the languages so good.

TOM.   *Eugh.*

MARIA.   Now this is the souvenir shop of Maria, and the offices of Dr. Fritz.

TOM.   *(Pain.)* Jesus Christ...!

MARIA.   *(Turning to look.)* Where?

TOM.   Is he here?

MARIA.   Jesus are everywhere.

TOM.   *Dr. Fritz.*

MARIA.   Oh, Dr. Fritz.

TOM.   Do you have a chair?

MARIA.   Only the chairs I am sitting on.

TOM.   Can I sit on it?

MARIA.   This is Dr. Fritz's chairs. Only Dr. Fritz can sit in this chairs.

TOM.   Wait a minute. *You're* not Dr. Fritz...?

MARIA.   I am the assistant of Dr. Fritz. *(Laughs madly. Then calm again.)* At the moment.

TOM.   Oh God ...

MARIA.   Good! You believe in God.

TOM.   What?

MARIA.   I say, Good! You believe in God.

TOM.   No I don't believe in God.

MARIA.   But *sinhors,* you called on God, you said, Oh God, oh God.

TOM.   It was a figure of speech, okay?

MARIA.   You believe in Buddha? Buddha is good.

TOM.   No.

MARIA.   Krishna, maybe?

TOM.   *No.*

MARIA.   Just checking. *(We hear a ringing.)*

TOM.   What's that?

MARIA.   What is what, *sinhors? (Ring.)*

TOM.   That ringing.

MARIA.   I hear nothings. *(Ring.)* Maybe the food poisoning make you a little *lo*coco. *(Ring.)*

TOM.   Don't you hear that bell?

MARIA.   Oh, the bells. *(Picks up doll and speaks into it like a telephone.) Mushi mushi ... Si ... Si ... Si ... Dosvee<u>don</u>yeh. (Hangs up the doll.)* That was Pedro the cook. He say you are on the way. *(Tom picks up the doll and looks at it.)* There is always more meat than meets the eyes meat, no?

TOM.   I must have fever.

MARIA.   Are you *shvitzing?*

TOM.   I am *shvitzing.*

MARIA.   This could be the fevers.

TOM.   Maria, look ...

MARIA.   Where?

TOM.   *Here.* Look *here.* If I die, tell them this.

MARIA.   We all will die, *sinhors* — God willing.

TOM.   Last night I ate supper at the hotel.

MARIA. The food was good?

TOM. *Eugh.*

MARIA. I am told it is good.

TOM. Middle of the night I thought I was going to die.

MARIA. You know I think this every day, but here I am. God willing.

TOM. Maria.

MARIA. *Si.*

TOM. I don't want Dr. Fritz anymore.

MARIA. No?

TOM. No. I just want to die.

MARIA. No, no, no, no, *sinhors.* Don't you see, the world are a great battle between the forces of the light, and the forces of the darkness. You must always stay on the side of the forces of light.

TOM. Look.... Please don't say where.

MARIA. I love you, Tom.

TOM. You what?

MARIA. Do you love me?

TOM. No.

MARIA. This is the unrequited love. No?

TOM. *Si.*

MARIA. God love you too.

TOM. I need a doctor! *(Phone ring.)*

MARIA. *(Picks up the doll and speaks into it.) Bon jour. Si. Si. Si. Si. No. Ciao. (Hangs up.)* This was God. He say you should believe in him.

TOM. Where is he?

MARIA. God? Upstairs.

TOM. *Dr. Fritz. Can I talk to Dr. Fritz? Please?*

MARIA. Of course you can talk to Dr. Fritz.

TOM. Okay. So where is he?

MARIA. You want to make an appointment?

TOM. I'm getting out of here. *(Starts out, but is stopped by pain.) Eugh.*

MARIA. Ah, but where will you go, *sinhors?* And how will you get there in your present conditions? *(Tom sinks down and lies on the floor.)*

TOM.   So this is where I'm going to die. I'm going to die here. I'm going to die!

MARIA/DR. FRITZ.   *Stille! Stille, du elender Hund! Du rückenloses Tier!* ["Quiet! You miserable dog! You spineless beast!"]

TOM.   What...?

MARIA/DR. FRITZ.   *Halt's Maul, du verfluchter Wurm! Oder sterben Sie! Na gut! Sterben Sie mal! Was geht das mich an?* ["Shut up, you confounded worm! Or else die! Go ahead! Die! What does it matter to me?"]

TOM.   What's going on here...?

MARIA/DR. FRITZ.   *(German accent.)* "I am dying, I am dying!" *Ja, ja,* perhaps you are dying. If I can shtop this dying I vill shtop it. I am not a magician. I am a physician. But you must listen, *ja?* You are listening? *Ja?*

TOM.   *Ja.*

MARIA/DR. FRITZ.   *Ja?*

TOM.   *Ja.*

MARIA/DR. FRITZ.   *Gut.* I am Dr. Fritz Ringsvwantd'l. How do you do.

TOM.   Dr. Rings ...

MARIA/DR. FRITZ.   Vwantd'l.

TOM.   Vandel.

MARIA/DR. FRITZ.   Vwantd'l.

TOM.   Vandel.

MARIA/DR. FRITZ.   Dr. Fritz. Okay?

TOM.   This is definitely fever ...

MARIA/DR. FRITZ.   *Also. Auf geht's.* ["So. Get up."]

TOM.   What?

MARIA/DR. FRITZ.   Shtand up on your footses.

TOM.   I — I can't ...

MARIA/DR. FRITZ.   *AUF GEHT'S, DU FAULER SCHWEIN! LOS! LOS!* ["Get up, you lazy pig! Move! Move!"] *(Tom gets up.)* "I can't get up!" You people. Too many Coca-Colas, it has eaten your brains. You haff no vill anymore. Too much of ze French fries mit ketchup at ze Golden Arches *von* MacDonald's.

TOM.   Can I sit in the chair?

MARIA/DR. FRITZ.   Ziss is Dr. Fritz's chairs. Only Dr. Fritz

can sit in ziss chairs. You — on the table zitzen. *Schnell! Schnell!*
["Fast! Fast!"] *(Tom sits on the table. Dr. Fritz takes out a pair of pliers.) Na gut.* Open wide.

TOM.   Open wide?

MARIA/DR. FRITZ.   You haff ze troothache?

TOM.   No.

MARIA/DR. FRITZ.   *Was?* I hear zere vas a man mit ze troothache.

TOM.   That's Pablo. I'm Tom.

MARIA/DR. FRITZ.   Who you are is not important, you mindless amoeba. *(Looks in each of Tom's eyes quickly.)* Zo. You haff ze conztipation, *ja?*

TOM.   I do have constipation.

MARIA/DR. FRITZ.   *Und* zometimes maybe you get a little prickly shtinging pain just behind ze *Ellenbogen*, hier, hmm? ["Ellenbogen" = "elbow."]

TOM.   I do get a little prickly pain right there.

MARIA/DR. FRITZ.   *Und* you haff ze very ugly dandruff.

TOM.   I do have dandruff.

MARIA/DR. FRITZ.   Zo I zee. You must use Head *und* Shoulders.

TOM.   I do use Head and Shoulders.

MARIA/DR. FRITZ.   Vunce a day, or tvice a day?

TOM.   Once.

MARIA/DR. FRITZ.   You must use this tvice a day and make ze good bubbly lather, *ja? Deine Hand.*

TOM.   What?

MARIA/DR. FRITZ.   Giff me your hand! *Schnell! (Takes Tom's hand and feels the pulse.)* Your pulse is normal.

TOM.   You're not wearing a watch.

MARIA/DR. FRITZ.   Your eyesight is excellent. Open your mouth. Stick out your tongue. Go like this. *(He makes a raspberry. Tom does too.)* No, like this. *(Another raspberry. Tom does too.)* Better. Now put your fingers in your ears. Can you hear me?

TOM.   What?

MARIA/DR. FRITZ.   Good. *(Slaps him on the top of the head.)*

TOM.   Ow!

MARIA/DR. FRITZ.   This hurts?

90

TOM.   Yes it hurts.

MARIA/DR. FRITZ.   A good sign. *(Takes out an ancient stethoscope.)* Lift ze blouse.

TOM.   Aren't you going to take my temperature?

MARIA/DR. FRITZ.   Ziss is a poor country, Meine Herren. I haff nothing here! Nothing! *(Feels Tom's forehead quickly.)* Besides — you haff no fever.

TOM.   But I'm shaking!

MARIA/DR. FRITZ.   Ziss is not fever. Ziss is shaking. Do you luff me?

TOM.   No!

MARIA/DR. FRITZ.   Vhy not?

TOM.   I don't know you.

MARIA/DR. FRITZ.   Good answer.

TOM.   Look —

MARIA/DR. FRITZ.   *(Looking behind.)* Vhere?

TOM.   *Eugh* ...

MARIA/DR. FRITZ.   You are sure you haff no troothache!

TOM.   I DON'T HAVE A GODDAMN TROOTHACHE!

MARIA/DR. FRITZ.   Just checking. But at four you had ze rheumatic fever. *Ja?*

TOM.   I did have the rheumatic fever ...

MARIA/DR. FRITZ.   At 13 you had ze doppel pneumonia and you thought you were going to die.

TOM.   I did.

MARIA/DR. FRITZ.   You died?

TOM.   I thought I was.

MARIA/DR. FRITZ.   You know, I thought this every day myself — then I did die.

TOM.   You died?

MARIA/DR. FRITZ.   I did. It vas August, 1912. I too vas on vacation. I too had a pain in my *eugh*. Suddenly, kaboom! I am dead.

TOM.   What was it like to die?

MARIA/DR. FRITZ.   I had better days. Now I must vander ze universe to complete my good verks.

TOM.   Wow.

MARIA/DR. FRITZ.   But I digress. Let's check your guts. At

15, you had ze ingrown toenail. For two weeks when you were 17 you had a rash on your buttocks in the shape of Santa Claus. At 20 you had rhinitis, bronchitis, conjunctivitis, and gonorrhea — a busy year for you. You zleep every day from 12:34 to 7:38 in the morning. You eat usually eggs and toast mit raspberry *shmier* for breakfast, ze garbage fast food for lunch, maybe ze wiener made from pig balls or a slice of *Scheisse* you call pizza. At ze nightimes you eat in a restaurant, sometimes Chinese, sometimes Italian, you haff ze gnocchis mit mushrooms *und* ze shmall green zalat.

TOM.   Amazing.

MARIA/DR. FRITZ.   Eleven forty-two at night you masturbate into a sock. Sometimes the argyle sock, sometimes the tube sock, sometimes the sock mit the clocks on the side.

TOM.   Good God.

MARIA/DR. FRITZ.   Ziss is your entire shtupid life.

TOM.   So what's wrong with me?

MARIA/DR. FRITZ.   I haff no idea. Lie down. *(Dr. Fritz straps Tom to the table.)*

TOM.   How do you know all these things about me?

MARIA/DR. FRITZ.   I am a highly qualified sturgeon.

TOM.   Surgeon.

MARIA/DR. FRITZ.   Sturgeon. Shmart guy.

TOM.   You know what's funny?

MARIA/DR. FRITZ.   I am German. Nothing is funny. Ha, ha, ha.

TOM.   I'm getting a troothache!

MARIA/DR. FRITZ.   Zympathetic reaction. You vant to buy a zoovenirs?

TOM.   No.

MARIA/DR. FRITZ.   Vun of a kinds.

TOM.   *OWW!*

MARIA/DR. FRITZ.   Na *ja.* Your case is not so complicated.

TOM.   What's wrong?

MARIA/DR. FRITZ.   You need an operation.

TOM.   An operation...?

MARIA/DR. FRITZ.   Immediately.

TOM.   You're kidding. Not here.

MARIA/DR. FRITZ.   Here.

TOM.   Not in this town.

MARIA/DR. FRITZ.   You zee another town?

TOM.   Not in this country.

MARIA/DR. FRITZ.   *(Produces some ugly-looking butcher knives.)* Unfortunately, I haff not the proper tools ...

TOM.   *(Struggling in the bands.)* No. No...!

MARIA/DR. FRITZ.   I haff no anesthetic, ziss could be quite painful. *(Starts sharpening one of the knives.)*

TOM.   But I'm fine! I'm fine!

MARIA/DR. FRITZ.   Fine? *Nein.*

TOM.   Will you undo these straps, please?

MARIA/DR. FRITZ.   The doctor is who, here?

TOM.   Who *is* the doctor here?

MARIA/DR. FRITZ.   *(American accent.)* I'm your mother, Tom. *(Tom screams.)* Does that make you feel better? *Also, das Messer.* *("So, the knife" — approaching Tom with the knife.)*

TOM.   Put that thing down!

MARIA/DR. FRITZ.   Perhaps for you ve need ze *besser Messer.* *(Takes out a bigger knife.)*

TOM.   I DON'T NEED A *MESSER!*

MARIA/DR. FRITZ.   Okay. You are fine? Then good. *(Undoes the straps.)* Go. You are free. I am not a torturer, I am a doctor. So go. Go! *(Tom gets up, turns and starts to go, but is stopped by a sudden pain that drops him to his knees.)*

TOM.   *Eugh. Eugh.* Oh God...!

MARIA/DR. FRITZ.   You believe in God?

TOM.   Suddenly I feel like total hell.

MARIA/DR. FRITZ.   *Ja,* you don't look too svell.

TOM.   I'm getting out of here. *(Tries to leave, but stops.)*

MARIA/DR. FRITZ.   But vhere vill you go? And how vill you get there in ziss conditions?

TOM.   *(Falling to the floor in pain.)* Eugh ...

MARIA/DR. FRITZ.   Do you not realize the place you have come to? The powers at verk, ze forces arrayed vhich could crush you like a peanut? *(Tom whimpers. Thunderclap.)* You haff finished your good verks, I hope.

TOM.   No! I haven't done anything! I ate hot dogs made

from pig balls and I had a rash on my butt and I jerk off into a sock every night!

MARIA/DR. FRITZ. Alas, now ze great battle is joined, Meine Herren, and you are in the middle of the field. Ze forces of light and ze forces of darkness are fighting for you. I only hope zatt you vill find your way to the forces of light very very soon.

TOM. But how?

MARIA/DR. FRITZ. A good kvestion. *(Phone ring.)* Ogh, ziss doll has been ringing off ze hook all day. *(Picks up the doll and speaks into it.)* Pronto. Si. Si. Si. Si. *(To Tom.)* It is for you.

TOM. For me...?

MARIA/DR. FRITZ. God vants to talk to you. *(Tom makes a gesture to say: "I'm not here.")* Here. Take it. Be nice. Ziss iss God.

TOM. *(Takes the doll and speaks into it.)* Hello...? Yes, this is he.... Fine. Actually, I'm not feeling so fine, I have a pain in my ... *(Realizing the pain is gone.)* Well, I *thought* I had a pain.... But listen, um, God, while I've got you on the line, maybe I could ask a few questions.... No, no, no, I understand, you've got other things. So great. I'll see you later — *much* later. I hope. Yes, it was nice talking to you, too. 'Bye. *(Puts the doll down.)*

MARIA. *(Hispanic again, knitting.)* How you are feeling *sinhors?*

TOM. I just talked to God...!

MARIA. You want to buy a souvenirs?

BLACKOUT

PROPERTY LIST

Knitting needles (MARIA)
Doll
Pliers (MARIA)
Old stethoscope (MARIA)
Ugly butcher knives (MARIA)

SOUND EFFECTS

Phone ringing
Thunder clap

DEGAS, C'EST MOI

DEGAS, C'EST MOI was presented as part of the Marathon '96 at Ensemble Studio Theatre (Curt Dempster, Artistic Director) in New York City, on May 8, 1996. It was directed by Shirley Kaplan; the set design was by Mike Allan; the costume design was by David K. Mickelsen; the lighting design was by Greg MacPherson; the sound design was by Jeffrey Taylor; and stage manager was Eileen Myers. The cast was as follows:

ED ....Don Berman
DORIS .... Susan Greenhill
MAN .... Chris Lutkin
WOMAN ....Ilene Kristen

this play is for Martha,
of course

DEGAS, C'EST MOI

Ed, on a bed, asleep. An alarm clock goes off. He doesn't move. Then, he is suddenly awake.

ED.   A stroke of genius. I decide to be Degas for a day. Edgar Degas. Why Degas? says a pesky little voice at the back of my head. Well why *not* Degas? *Pourquoi pas* Degas? Maybe the prismatic bars of color on my ceiling have inspired me. *(We see prismatic bars of color.)* Maybe the creamy white light spreading on my walls has moved me. *(Creamy white light spreads on the wall.)* Maybe it's all this cheap French wine I been drinking. *(He finds a bottle in his bed.)* But yes! Today I will be Edgar Degas! — Is it Ed*gar,* or Ed*ouard?* Okay, so I don't know much about Degas. Let's see. Dead, French, impressionist painter of, what, jockeys, ballerinas, flowers, that kinda thing. And okay granted, I'm not French, dead, or a painter of any kind. Not a lotta common ground. And yet, and yet — are Degas and I not united by our shared humanity? By our common need for love, coffee, and deodorant?

DORIS.   Oh God, oh God, oh God. Have you seen my glasses?

ED.   Doris breaks in on my inspiration.

DORIS.   I can't find my glasses.

ED.   Doris, I say to Doris, I'm going to be Degas today.

DORIS.   He's gonna kill me if I'm late again.

ED.   Doris doesn't see the brilliance of the idea.

DORIS.   This is a tragedy.

ED.   Doris — I am Degas!

DORIS.   You're what?

ED.   Is it Edgar or Edward? It's Edgar, isn't it.

DORIS.   Don't forget the dry cleaning. *(Doris kisses him.)* 'Bye. *(Doris exits.)*

ED. Alas, poor Doris. Distracted by the banal. No matter. I start my day and brush my teeth as Degas. *(Ed produces a green toothbrush.)* Oh man. This is wonderful! In the bathroom, everything seems transfigured, yet nothing has changed. The very porcelain pullulates with possibilities. Will you look at the lustre of that toilet? And the light on that green plastic! The bristles are disgusting, but the light is fantastic! *(French accent:)* Per'aps I weel paint you later. *(We hear the sound of shower running.)* In the shower, it feels strange, lathering an immortal. What's even stranger, the immortal is lathering back. How did I become such a genius? I, who flunked woodshop in high school? Was it my traumatic childhood? Did I *have* a traumatic childhood? There was Uncle Stosh's unfortunate party trick with the parakeet. *Ouch.* Well something must've happened. Because now I'm great. I'm brilliant. My name will live forever! *(He considers that a second.)* Whoo. Wow. This is too big for even me to contemplate. I go out into the world with dry cleaning. *(He grabs some clothing as we hear city noises, car horns, etcetera.)* O glorious polychromatic city! Gone the dreary daily déjà vu. Today — *Degas* vu! *(A Car Driver enters at a run, holding a steering wheel, headed right for Ed. Loud car horn and screeching brakes heard as Ed dodges aside.)*

DRIVER. Moron!

ED. Idiot!

DRIVER. Jerk! Watch where you're going!

ED. Do you know who you almost killed?

DRIVER. Yeah! An *asshole!* *(Driver exits.)*

ED. Another couple of inches and the world would've lost a hundred masterpieces. *(Dry Cleaner enters, writing on a pad.)*

DRY CLEANER. Okay what's the dirt today?

ED. At the dry cleaners' I notice something strange …

DRY CLEANER. *(Taking the dry cleaning.)* One shirt, one skirt, one jacket.

ED. My dry cleaner acts exactly the same.

DRY CLEANER. You know you need some serious reweaving?

ED. Madam, how I would love to capture you in charcoal.

DRY CLEANER. My husband already caught me in puce. *(Tears a sheet off the pad.)* After five. *(The Dry Cleaner exits with the clothing.)*

ED.   She gives not a flutter of recognition. Then on the corner, the newsguy tries to sell me my paper just like always. *(Newsguy enters.)*

NEWSGUY.   *Daily Noose?*

ED.   Actually, have you got anything *en française?*

NEWSGUY.   Let's see, I got *Le Mot, Le Monde, Le Reve, Le Chat, La Chasse, L'Abime* and *Mademoiselle Boom Boom.*

ED.   I'll just take the *News.*

NEWSGUY.   Change. *(He flips an invisible coin, which Ed "catches," then the Newsguy exits.)*

ED.   Still not a blink of recognition. Then as I head down Broadway, people pass me by without a second glance. Or even a first glance. *(People enter and pass him.)* I might as well be invisible. I, Edgar Degas! And then I realize with a shock: *it makes no difference to be Degas.* To all these people, I could be anyone! And if I'm anyone — who are all these people? *(More people pass him.)* And yet.... And yet maybe the other Degas walked this invisibly through Paris. *(We hear a French accordion.)* Maybe he too was rudely bumped into by the bourgeoisie on the upper Left Bank ... *(A Pedestrian bumps into him as a Worker enters carrying a crate loaded with cabbages.)* Shouted at by workers at the Key Food *de Montparnasse* ...

WORKER.   Watcha back, watcha back! *(Worker exits.)*

ED.   Cursed by the less fortunate. *(Homeless Person enters.)*

HOMELESS PERSON.   *Fuck* you. *Fuck* you.

ED.   And you know, there's a kind of comfort in this.

HOMELESS PERSON.   *Fuck* you.

ED.   Completely anonymous, I'm free to appreciate the grey cloud of pigeons overhead ... *(We hear the cooing of pigeons.)* The impasto at Ray's Pizza....

VOICE OF PIZZA MAN.   *Pepperoni!*

ED.   The chiaroscuro of the M-Eleven bus. *(Loud motor of a city bus.)* Nobody knows it, but I am walking down this street with a jewel cupped in my hands. The secret precious jewel of my talent. *(Unemployment Worker enters.)*

UNEMPLOYMENT WORKER.   Next!

ED.   My delicious anonymity continues at Unemployment. *(A sign descends: "UNEMPLOYMENT LINE HERE.")*

UNEMPLOYMENT WORKER. Sign your claim at the bottom, please.

ED. Do you notice the name I signed in the bottom right corner?

UNEMPLOYMENT WORKER. Edgar Day-hass. Edgar Deejis. Edgar Deggis. Edgar De Gas. Edgar De What?

ED. Edgar Degas. And — ?

UNEMPLOYMENT WORKER. *And* — this name at the bottom does not match the name at the top of the form.

ED. No, no, no, no ...

UNEMPLOYMENT WORKER. Are you not the same person as the person at the top of the form?

ED. I am a person at the top of *my* form. I am *Edgar. Degas.*

UNEMPLOYMENT WORKER. The dead French painter?

ED. The same.

UNEMPLOYMENT WORKER. Next! *(Unemployment Worker exits and the sign goes away.)*

ED. Recalling my painterly interest in racetracks, I stop off at OTB. *(OTB Worker enters.)*

OTB WORKER. Next!

ED. Ten francs on Windmill, *s'il vous plait.*

OTB WORKER. Oh *mais oui,* monsieur.

ED. Windmill — I say to him — because the jockey wears brilliant silks of crimson and gold. Windmill — I tell the man — because her sable flanks flash like lightning in the field. Windmill — I continue — because in form and moving she doth express an angel.

OTB WORKER. *(Handing over the betting slip.)* Windmill —

ED. — he says to me —

OTB WORKER. — always comes in last. *(Racing bell.)*

ED. And Windmill does. *(Buzzer.)* But who gives a shit? *(Tears up the betting slip.)* I'm Degas! *(OTB Worker exits. Ed looks around.)* Oh — the library. Maybe I should look myself up. *(A sign descends: "Silence." A Librarian enters.)*

LIBRARIAN. *Shhhhhh!*

ED. Excuse me. Have you got anything on Degas?

LIBRARIAN. Degas. You mean the crassly conservative counterfeminist patriarchal pedophile painter?

ED.   No, I mean the colorist who chronicled his age and who continues to inspire through countless posters, postcards and T-shirts.

LIBRARIAN.   Section D, aisle 2.

ED.   Patriarchal pedoph ...

LIBRARIAN.   *QUIET! (Librarian exits.)*

ED.   But who needs the carping of critics, the lies of biographers? I know who I am. And, famished by creativity, I stop at Twin Donut. *(Two tables appear. A Young Woman sits at one, writing in a journal. Ed sits at the other.)*

TWIN DONUT WORKER.   *(Enters with a plate.)* Vanilla cruller! *(Exits.)*

ED.   So there I am, scribbling a priceless doodle on my napkin when I notice someone staring at me. *(The Young Woman stops writing and looks at Ed.)* A young woman writing in a journal. Has she recognized me? She smiles slightly. Yes. She knows I am Degas. Not only that. *(He looks again. The Young Woman starts writing.)* She *loves* Degas. That one look has redeemed all my years of effort. My work has given meaning to someone's life. Should I seduce her? It would be traditional. *(A schmaltzy-romantic violin is heard.)*

YOUNG WOMAN.   *(Writing.)* "April six. Twin Donut. Just saw Edgar Degas two tables over. So he likes vanilla crullers too! Suddenly this day is glorious and memorable. Would love to lie in bed all afternoon and make *l'amour* with Degas ..."

ED.   But no. I'd only cast her off, break her heart. Not to mention what it would do to Doris.

YOUNG WOMAN.   "Dwayne would kill me."

ED.   But isn't it my duty as an artist to seduce this girl? Experience life to the fullest...?

YOUNG WOMAN.   Adieu.

ED.   Adieu. *(Young Woman exits.)* Too late. *(Tables disappear. Afternoon light.)* On Fifth Avenue, a mysterious figure passes, leading a Doberman. Or vice versa. *(A Figure in a raincoat, hat and sunglasses, holding a stiffened leash, as if a dog were on it, crosses.)* It's somebody famous. But who? Kissinger? Woody Allen? Roseanne? *(Figure exits.)* Whoa, whoa, whoa, just for a picosecond there, I forget who I am! Just for a moment — I seem to be nobody. The labor of hanging onto one's identity! *(Empty picture frames descend and a Museum Guard enters.)* At the museum I am simply amazed to find how much I accomplished — even without television. *(Degas self-portrait appears.)* What's this…. Ah. A self-portrait. Not a great likeness, maybe. But so full of … what? … *feeling*. I stare into my fathomless eyes. *(A Museumgoer stands beside him looking at the portrait.)*

MUSEUMGOER.   Mmm.

ED.   Mmmmmmm.

MUSEUMGOER.   Bit smudgy, isn't it?

ED.   "Smudgy"?

MUSEUMGOER.   This area in here.

ED.   Yeah, but what about this area over here?

MUSEUMGOER.   No, but look at this area here.

ED.   Okay. So I had an off day.

MUSEUMGOER.   An "off day"…?

ED.   Not all my work was perfect.

MUSEUMGOER.   Indeed. How could it be…? *(The Museumgoer slips away.)*

ED.   Philistine. Probably headed for Van Gogh. To kneel in adoration at the sunflowers. I couldn't believe it, the day he started signing his paintings "Vincent." "Vince," we called him. What a jerk. *(Degas's "Woman with Chrysanthemums" appears.)* Ah yes. "Woman with Chrysanthemums." A personal favorite among my masterworks. God, when I remember that morning over a century ago…. Can it be that long now? This was an empty canvas and I stood in front it paralyzed by its whiteness. Then I reached for my brush … *(He produces a paintbrush.)* … and the picture crystallized. In a moment I saw it all. This pensive woman, oblivious of the transcendent burst of color right at her shoulder. The natural exuberance of the flowers alongside her human sorrow. Yes! Yes! Our blindness to the beautiful! Our insensibility to the splendor right there within our reach!

MUSEUM GUARD.   Step back, please.

ED.   Excuse me?

MUSEUM GUARD.   You have to step back, sir. You're too

close to the painting.

ED.   I'm too close to this painting...?

MUSEUM GUARD.   Do you copy?

ED.   I never copy. I am an original!

MUSEUM GUARD.   Sir?

ED.   I step back. *(He does so, and the Museum Guard exits.)* But the glow of my exaltation stays with me all the way to the Akropolis diner ... *(A table. Doris enters.)*

DORIS.   Oh God, oh God.

ED.   ... where Doris meets me for dinner.

DORIS.   What a day.

ED.   What a fabulous day. Epic!

DORIS.   Six hours of Xeroxing.

ED.   No, listen. Degas. Remember?

DORIS.   Degas...?

ED.   I've been Degas today.

DORIS.   The toilets erupted again. The women's room was like Vesuvius.

ED.   I *am* Degas.

DORIS.   They were going to fix those toilets last week.

ED.   As Doris dilates on toilets, I begin to feel Degas slip away a little ...

DORIS.   Waiter!

ED.   ... like a second skin I'm shedding ...

DORIS.   Waiter!

ED.   ... leaving nothing behind.

DORIS.   Where is that guy?

ED.   Then I see a man at another table, staring at me. Looking at me with such pity. Such unalloyed human sympathy.

DORIS.   At least I found my glasses.

ED.   And then I realize.

DORIS.   They were in my purse all the time.

ED.   The man is Renoir.

DORIS.   *(Holding up her glasses.)* See?

ED.   By now, Degas is completely gone. *(Light changes to night light as Ed and Doris rise.)* Doris and I walk home in silence. *(Doris exits. Lights darken to a single spot on Ed.)* People say they have a voice inside their heads. The voice that tells themselves

107

the story of their lives. Now I'm walking up the street, now I'm taking out my key, when did that streetlight burn out, is there a meaning to all this, who's that person coming down the stairs, now I'm putting my key in the door, now I do this, now I do that. The facts of our lives. Yes, I too have always had a voice like that in my head. But now, tonight, no one is listening. That presence that always listened in at the back of my mind is no longer there. Nor is there a presence behind that presence listening in. Nor a presence behind that, nor behind that, nor behind that. All the way back to the back of my mind, no one is listening in. The story of my life is going on unwatched. Unheard. I am alone. *(The bed appears.)* I find myself upstairs, sprawled on the bed while Doris runs the bathwater. Degas is dust. All my glory, all my fame, all my achievements are utterly forgotten. Immortality? A cruel joke. The jewel I bore through the streets in the cup of my hands is gone, and my hands are empty. I have done nothing. Absolutely nothing. *(A light comes up on Doris, drying herself with a towel.)* Then I find myself looking through the doorway into the bathroom and I see Doris standing naked with her foot up on the edge of the old lion-footed tub, drying herself. The overhead light is dim, but Doris is fluorescent — radiant — luminous — with pinks and lavenders and vermillions playing over her skin. The frayed towel she's wrapped in gleams like a rose. She turns and looks back at me and smiles. *(Doris turns and looks over her shoulder at Ed.)*

DORIS.   *Bon soir,* Degas.

ED.   Degas...! Who needs him? *(He holds his hand out to her across the intervening space, and she holds hers out to him.)*

LIGHTS FADE

PROPERTY LIST

Wine bottle (ED)
Green toothbrush (ED)
Clothing (ED)
Steering wheel (CAB DRIVER)
Pad of dry cleaning receipts (DRY CLEANER)
Newspapers (NEWSGUY)
Crate of cabbages (WORKER)
Sign: "UNEMPLOYMENT LINE HERE"
Betting slip (OTB WORKER)
Sign: "SILENCE"
Journal and pencil or pen (YOUNG WOMAN)
Plate with vanilla cruller (TWIN DONUT WORKER)
Pen or pencil (DEGAS)
Napkin (TWIN DONUT WORKER)
Stiffened leash (FIGURE)
Empty picture frames
Degas self-portrait
"Women with Chrysanthemums" painting
Paintbrush (ED)
Eyeglasses (DORIS)
Towel (DORIS)

SOUND EFFECTS

Alarm clock
Shower running
City noises
Car horn
Loud car horn
Screeching brakes
French accordion
Cooing of pigeons
Loud motor of a city bus
Racing bell
Buzzer
Romantic violin

NEW PLAYS

★ **MATCH by Stephen Belber.** Mike and Lisa Davis interview a dancer and choreographer about his life, but it is soon evident that their agenda will either ruin or inspire them—and definitely change their lives forever. "Prolific laughs and ear-to-ear smiles." –*NY Magazine.* "Uproariously funny, deeply moving, enthralling theater. Stephen Belber's MATCH has great beauty and tenderness, and abounds in wit." –*NY Daily News.* "Three and a half out of four stars." –*USA Today.* "A theatrical steeplechase that leads straight from outrageous bitchery to unadorned, heartfelt emotion." –*Wall Street Journal.* [2M, 1W] ISBN: 0-8222-2020-2

★ **HANK WILLIAMS: LOST HIGHWAY by Randal Myler and Mark Harelik.** The story of the beloved and volatile country-music legend Hank Williams, featuring twenty-five of his most unforgettable songs. "[LOST HIGHWAY has] the exhilarating feeling of Williams on stage in a particular place on a particular night…serves up classic country with the edges raw and the energy hot…By the end of the play, you've traveled on a profound emotional journey: LOST HIGHWAY transports its audience and communicates the inspiring message of the beauty and richness of Williams' songs…forceful, clear-eyed, moving, impressive." –*Rolling Stone.* "…honors a very particular musical talent with care and energy… smart, sweet, poignant." –*NY Times.* [7M, 3W] ISBN: 0-8222-1985-9

★ **THE STORY by Tracey Scott Wilson.** An ambitious black newspaper reporter goes against her editor to investigate a murder and finds the *best* story…but at what cost? "A singular new voice…deeply emotional, deeply intellectual, and deeply musical…" –*The New Yorker.* "…a conscientious and absorbing new drama…" –*NY Times.* "…a riveting, tough-minded drama about race, reporting and the truth…" –*A.P.* "… a stylish, attention-holding script that ends on a chilling note that will leave viewers with much to talk about." –*Curtain Up.* [2M, 7W (doubling, flexible casting)] ISBN: 0-8222-1998-0

★ **OUR LADY OF 121st STREET by Stephen Adly Guirgis.** The body of Sister Rose, beloved Harlem nun, has been stolen, reuniting a group of life-challenged childhood friends who square off as they wait for her return. "A scorching and dark new comedy… Mr. Guirgis has one of the finest imaginations for dialogue to come along in years." –*NY Times.* "Stephen Guirgis may be the best playwright in America under forty." –*NY Magazine.* [8M, 4W] ISBN: 0-8222-1965-4

★ **HOLLYWOOD ARMS by Carrie Hamilton and Carol Burnett.** The coming-of-age story of a dreamer who manages to escape her bleak life and follow her romantic ambitions to stardom. Based on Carol Burnett's bestselling autobiography, *One More Time.* "…pure theatre and pure entertainment…" –*Talkin' Broadway.* "…a warm, fuzzy evening of theatre." –*BrodwayBeat.com.* "…chuckles and smiles of recognition or surprise flow naturally…a remarkable slice of life." –*TheatreScene.net.* [5M, 5W, 1 girl] ISBN: 0-8222-1959-X

★ **INVENTING VAN GOGH by Steven Dietz.** A haunting and hallucinatory drama about the making of art, the obsession to create and the fine line that separates truth from myth. "Like a van Gogh painting, Dietz's story is a gorgeous example of excess—one that remakes reality with broad, well-chosen brush strokes. At evening's end, we're left with the author's resounding opinions on art and artifice, and provoked by his constant query into which is greater: van Gogh's art or his violent myth." –*Phoenix New Times.* "Dietz's writing is never simple. It is always brilliant. Shaded, compressed, direct, lucid—he frames his subject with a remarkable understanding of painting as a physical experience." –*Tucson Citizen.* [4M, 1W] ISBN: 0-8222-1954-9

DRAMATISTS PLAY SERVICE, INC.
440 Park Avenue South, New York, NY 10016   212-683-8960   Fax 212-213-1539
postmaster@dramatists.com   www.dramatists.com

NEW PLAYS

★ **INTIMATE APPAREL by Lynn Nottage.** The moving and lyrical story of a turn-of-the-century black seamstress whose gifted hands and sewing machine are the tools she uses to fashion her dreams from the whole cloth of her life's experiences. "...Nottage's play has a delicacy and eloquence that seem absolutely right for the time she is depicting..." –*NY Daily News.* "...thoughtful, affecting...The play offers poignant commentary on an era when the cut and color of one's dress—and of course, skin—determined whom one could and could not marry, sleep with, even talk to in public." –*Variety.* [2M, 4W] ISBN: 0-8222-2009-1

★ **BROOKLYN BOY by Donald Margulies.** A witty and insightful look at what happens to a writer when his novel hits the bestseller list. "The characters are beautifully drawn, the dialogue sparkles..." –*nytheatre.com.* "Few playwrights have the mastery to smartly investigate so much through a laugh-out-loud comedy that combines the vintage subject matter of successful writer-returning-to-ethnic-roots with the familiar mid-life crisis." –*Show Business Weekly.* [4M, 3W] ISBN: 0-8222-2074-1

★ **CROWNS by Regina Taylor.** Hats become a springboard for an exploration of black history and identity in this celebratory musical play. "Taylor pulls off a Hat Trick: She scores thrice, turning CROWNS into an artful amalgamation of oral history, fashion show, and musical theater..." –*TheatreMania.com.* "...wholly theatrical...Ms. Taylor has created a show that seems to arise out of spontaneous combustion, as if a bevy of department-store customers simultaneously decided to stage a revival meeting in the changing room." –*NY Times.* [1M, 6W (2 musicians)] ISBN: 0-8222-1963-8

★ **EXITS AND ENTRANCES by Athol Fugard.** The story of a relationship between a young playwright on the threshold of his career and an aging actor who has reached the end of his. "[Fugard] can say more with a single line than most playwrights convey in an entire script...Paraphrasing the title, it's safe to say this drama, making its memorable entrance into our consciousness, is unlikely to exit as long as a theater exists for exceptional work." –*Variety.* "A thought-provoking, elegant and engrossing new play..." –*Hollywood Reporter.* [2M] ISBN: 0-8222-2041-5

★ **BUG by Tracy Letts.** A thriller featuring a pair of star-crossed lovers in an Oklahoma City motel facing a bug invasion, paranoia, conspiracy theories and twisted psychological motives. "...obscenely exciting...top-flight craftsmanship. Buckle up and brace yourself..." –*NY Times.* "...[a] thoroughly outrageous and thoroughly entertaining play...the possibility of enemies, real and imagined, to squash has never been more theatrical." –*A.P.* [3M, 2W] ISBN: 0-8222-2016-4

★ **THOM PAIN (BASED ON NOTHING) by Will Eno.** An ordinary man muses on childhood, yearning, disappointment and loss, as he draws the audience into his last-ditch plea for empathy and enlightenment. "It's one of those treasured nights in the theater—treasured nights anywhere, for that matter—that can leave you both breathless with exhilaration and...in a puddle of tears." –*NY Times.* "Eno's words...are familiar, but proffered in a way that is constantly contradictory to our expectations. Beckett is certainly among his literary ancestors." –*nytheatre.com.* [1M] ISBN: 0-8222-2076-8

★ **THE LONG CHRISTMAS RIDE HOME by Paula Vogel.** Past, present and future collide on a snowy Christmas Eve for a troubled family of five. "...[a] lovely and hauntingly original family drama...a work that breathes so much life into the theater." –*Time Out.* "...[a] delicate visual feast..." –*NY Times.* "...brutal and lovely...the overall effect is magical." –*NY Newsday.* [3M, 3W] ISBN: 0-8222-2003-2

DRAMATISTS PLAY SERVICE, INC.
440 Park Avenue South, New York, NY 10016 212-683-8960 Fax 212-213-1539
postmaster@dramatists.com www.dramatists.com